The WORST-CASE SCENARIO

SURVIVE-O-PEDIA

JUNIOR EDITION

BY DAVID BORGENICHT, MOLLY SMITH,
BRENDAN WALSH, AND ROBIN EPSTEIN
ILLUSTRATED BY CHUCK GONZALES

chronicle books·san francisco

A WORD OF WARNING: It's always important to keep safety in mind. If you're careless, even the tamest activities can result in injury. As such, all readers are urged to act with caution, ask for adult advice, obey all laws, and respect the rights of others when handling any Worst-Case Scenario.

Library of Congress Cataloging-in-Publication Data available.
ISBN 978-0-8118-7690-2

Cover design by Stislow Design + Illustration.
Book design by Lynne Yeamans.
Typeset in Adobe Garamond, Blockhead, Broadletter JNL, Imperfect, and Indecision.
Illustrations © Chuck Gonzales.

Front cover photo: © Image Source/Corbis (shark)

Back cover photos: © iStockphoto.com/Patricia Hofmeester (rocks);
iStockphoto.com/Alistair Forrester Shankie (rocks);
© iStockphoto.com/Ameng Wu (snake)

Manufactured by Toppan Leefung, Da Ling Shan Town, Dongguan, China, in April 2011.

1 3 5 7 9 10 8 6 4 2

Chronicle Books LLC
680 Second Street, San Francisco, California 94107

www.chroniclekids.com

CONTENTS

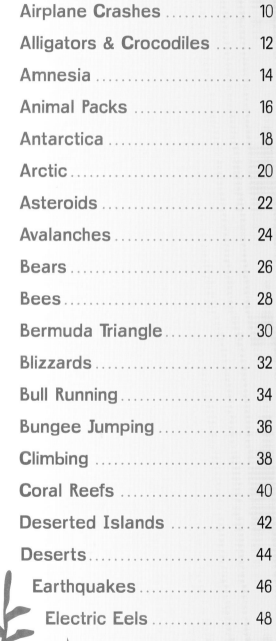

INTRODUCTON

The captain's soothing voice announces over the loudspeaker: "Ladies and gentlemen, we've reached our cruising altitude." Time to sit back, relax, and watch the in-flight movie. But it smells like something's burning. You look out your window…uh-oh, your plane's engine is on fire!

Your best chance for survival is to grab a parachute and take a flying leap. Three, two, one…jump! Phew, the hardest part is over. You're out of that airplane and soaring like an eagle. Now you just need to open your chute and glide back to Earth. You hit the parachute's release button, but oh no—it doesn't open! Luckily, you spot a fellow jumper and grab hold! Don't relax yet—a gust of wind blows you out to sea. Fortunately, you avoid the open water and land on the deck of a ship. Wait, this ship is sinking! Now, you're bobbing in shark-infested waters, so you'd better start swimming fast to that deserted island up ahead. Too bad its volcano is about to erupt! Of course, you'll worry about that *after* you dodge the *hissing* komodo dragon that's come to greet you as you wade ashore…

But don't panic!

Of course, panicking may seem like the natural response to all of these extreme situations, but it turns out that *keeping your cool* is an incredibly important key to your survival. And you're holding the other key in your hands right now! Reading this *Survive-o-Pedia* will help prepare you for life's "little" disasters. And we don't mean forgetting your locker combination. We're talking about dealing with catastrophes of avalanche-type proportions, like, well, an avalanche.

As you'll soon find out, being armed with lots of knowledge is your first—and often best—line of defense, whether you're dealing with a charging bull, an angry mob, a trembling earthquake, or anything else that might shake you to your core. Each entry in this book gives you the information you need to prepare for and survive extreme situations that can strike close to home (like lightning) and that can hit when you're far afield (like an iceberg).

But this book's not just a survival guide. It's also an encyclopedia chock-full of fun facts about extreme conditions and situations. Did you know that the box jellyfish kills more people annually than any other marine animal? Or that Antarctica is drier than the Sahara desert? How about elevators being able to fall up as well as plummet down? You *will* know soon enough.

And on top of all that, it's packed with photos and illustrations that make you feel like you're smack-dab in the middle of the action—without having to experience any skin-ripping bite marks yourself. Think of it as all of the adventure with none of the stitches!

Survive-o-Pedia covers natural disasters, wild animal encounters, travel dangers, and even extreme sports. So by the end of this book—with all you've seen and learned—you'll be ready to hike the densest woods, climb the highest mountains, explore the hottest deserts, and navigate the lushest jungles, while potentially dealing with malaria, killer bees, and angry gorillas. In other words, you'll be diving into the worst of the *worst* worst-case scenarios, *and* living to tell about it.

Whether you're in the mood for heart-pounding adventure or you want to stare down that which scares you, this book will not only help you reach the summit, it will also help you get safely back down. The world is yours to experience, and with *Survive-o-Pedia* as your guide, you'll be mentally equipped to handle anything!

AIRPLANE CRASHES

If you think about it, it's freaky to soar above the clouds in a heavy metal container. But it's even freakier to think about falling down to the ground. (OK, *don't* think about that!) Since most plane crashes actually occur closer to the ground—at take-off and landing—the following safety strategies can help improve your chances of walking away unscathed.

Seat Yourself

While you're boarding the plane, check out where the emergency exits are. If you can, choose an aisle seat. That way you have an easier route for escape (and you won't have to climb over strangers every time you have to pee). Also, airplanes typically crash nose first, so if you sit toward the rear of the plane, you can increase your odds of survival. First class might be the priciest section of the plane, but coach is the safest. Who needs all of that extra legroom anyway?

Count On It

After you take your seat, read the airplane's safety card. Pay attention when the flight attendant explains the aircraft's safety features. Then count the number of rows between you and the two nearest exits, just in case the path to one of them is blocked. If the plane does crash, it could be dark or smoky. You can then count off the number of rows with your hands to reach the exit.

FAST FACT

The odds of surviving a plane crash may be better than you think. Officially, 95 percent of passengers in airplane accidents survive.

OPPOSITE PAGE: US Airways Flight 1549, aka the "Miracle on the Hudson," has a safe landing on the Hudson River in New York, United States, on January 15, 2009.

HOW TO SURVIVE A PLANE CRASH

1 **Duck and cover.** If you're crashing, you'll know it. Tighten your seat belt and bend forward with one arm across your knees. If you have a pillow, place it in your lap and hold your head against it with your free arm.

2 **Brace for impact.** Place your feet or your knees directly against the seat in front of you. If you are over water, be ready for two big jolts: when the plane first hits the water and when the nose hits the water again.

3 **Get out!** Now that you've survived the crash, stay calm but act quickly. Leave everything behind and get out as fast as you can. If it's a water landing, you generally have less than two minutes to safely exit before the plane begins to sink. If you are on land, get as far away from the plane as possible in case of an explosion.

DON'T

DO

ALLIGATORS & CROCODILES

If you find yourself eyeball to eyeball with one of the world's largest reptiles, you might not want to spend time determining if you're looking at a 2,500 pound (1,134 kg) crocodile or a 1,000 pound (454 kg) alligator. But learning their key differences is important because you'll want all the facts when trying to outwit a killer *crocodilian*!

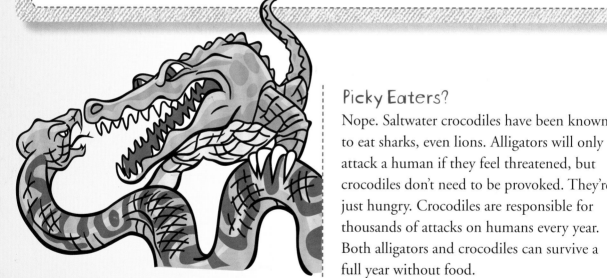

Check Out the Snout

Crocodiles have a V-shaped snout with the fourth tooth on the lower jaw sticking out and pointing up. The alligator's snout is wide and U-shaped and packs more bone-crushing power than a crocodile's—it uses this power to crack turtle shells with a single snap. By the way, the fourth tooth on a gator is not visible.

Picky Eaters?

Nope. Saltwater crocodiles have been known to eat sharks, even lions. Alligators will only attack a human if they feel threatened, but crocodiles don't need to be provoked. They're just hungry. Crocodiles are responsible for thousands of attacks on humans every year. Both alligators and crocodiles can survive a full year without food.

Good Old-Timers

Ancestors of today's alligators and crocodiles were around about two hundred million years ago. That's before most dinosaurs! A saltwater crocodile today can live to seventy years of age, while the American alligator has a maximum lifespan of about fifty years.

BE AWARE • In the small country of Burundi in Africa, a serial killer lurks. His name is Gustave, and he is an extra-large freshwater crocodile. Gustave is feared by the locals and is believed to have killed 200 people.

HOW TO AVOID AN ATTACK

1 Steer clear. In an area where there are crocs or gators, stay at least 20 feet (6 m) away from the water. They've been known to jump that far to snag prey. Gators (and crocs) are masters of the surprise attack from the water.

2 Kick into high gear. Though they are not known to chase down prey on land, crocs and gators are capable of short bursts of speed up to 10 miles (16 km) per hour. So stay at least 35 feet (11 m) away if you see one on land. If a gator does charge, you can outrun it, because it won't chase you for long. But don't get tricky. Remember that the shortest distance between two points is a straight line.

3 Punch it. If a gator or croc does happen to grab hold of something (like your leg!), give it a tap or punch on the snout. These creatures are known to open their mouths when tapped lightly.

AMNESIA ???

Ever snapped awake from a deep sleep and not known where you were, how you got there, or if you were really awake or still dreaming? Now imagine that feeling not going away. That's sort of what amnesia feels like. And it can last for hours...days...or even years!

Bonk!

Post-traumatic amnesia is the most common type and can be caused by a head injury from something like a car accident or a sports collision. There are two major types of amnesia: retrograde and anterograde. With retrograde amnesia, you can't remember anything that happened before the accident; with anterograde, you can remember what happened before the accident, but you can't make any new memories. Either way, it's not fun!

Where Am I?

Transient global amnesia can occur out of nowhere. With these rare cases, victims cannot remember where they are or how they got there. Even if they figure out what's going on, they forget it again. They can remember their names and recognize people they know, but they can't recall things that happened even a few minutes earlier. One symptom of this kind of amnesia is that people will repeat the exact same thing every two minutes or so.

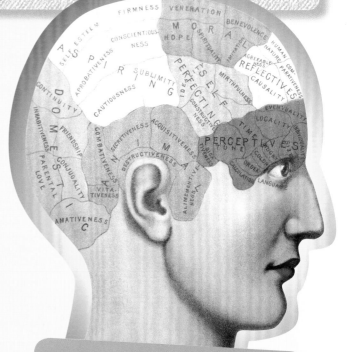

BE AWARE • Retrograde amnesiacs don't forget everything they know. They may not be able to remember people, places, or things they've done, but they often remember motor skills, like tying a shoelace, riding a bike, or even playing the piano.

Total Recall

Luckily, a sudden attack of amnesia only lasts for about twenty-four hours. Scientists aren't sure what causes these sudden attacks, but theories involve a loss of blood flow to the brain, a seizure, or a kind of migraine headache. If the amnesia was caused by a head injury, however, it can take a lot longer to recover. The hippocampus in the temporal lobe of the brain processes our memories. When amnesiacs do snap out of it, they usually remember older memories first.

OTHER FORGETFUL AFFLICTIONS

Face Blindness. People with this have normal vision, but they can't identify a person by their face alone. They need to hear a voice. Often, they can't even recognize a picture of themselves.

Visual Agnosia. People with this affliction will mistake an object, like a parking meter, for a person, or mistake a person for an object, like a hat.

Hearing Choresia. People, usually kids, with this disorder cannot make sense of words that relate to performing household chores. "Clean your room!" "Huh?"

Have we met?

ANIMAL PACKS

If you are surrounded by a pack of wild dogs, dingoes, coyotes, or wolves, you won't win them over by offering up some belly rubs. They might look like dogs, but they only know one way to get their food—and it isn't from a doggy bowl. Here's how to crack the pack.

Mean Streets?

The city of Moscow in Russia is overrun by packs of wild dogs—35,000 strays live on the streets. In 2008, there were 20,000 cases of attacks by wild dogs on people, and 8,000 of these attacks were serious enough to need police or medical attention. In order to survive, the strays need to be quite clever. Some can even navigate the subway system. Packs have been known to send the cutest dog of the bunch out to do the group's begging.

Alpha Pair

You may have heard the term "alpha male" before. But in a pack of wolves, it's actually an alpha *pair* that dominates. These two wolves, a male and a female, mate for life and the rest of the pack is mostly made up of their offspring. Some experts say we shouldn't use the term "alpha" at all, because they don't fight their way to the top. They get their authority just by being mom and dad.

Dingo-ing, Going...

The dingo is a wild dog and pack animal native to Australia. Long considered a nuisance, especially to farmers, the dingo is now on the verge of extinction. Because dingoes are a threat to livestock, farmers are permitted by the government to kill them. Dingoes are also breeding with wild dogs. Perhaps as little as 20 percent of the dingo population remains purebred.

Fighting rarely occurs among wolves, as they understand their rank within the pack.

HOW TO AVOID A WOLF PACK ATTACK

1 **Stay still.** Refrain from running. Wolves can run as fast as 35 miles (56 km) per hour. You can't.

2 **Give a holler.** If a wolf has its tail straight up in the air and its ears pricked, this means it might be getting ready to charge. What should you do? Give your best battle cry.

3 **Charge!** Pick a wolf—perhaps the smallest one—and charge at it first. It might sound crazy, but wolves have a strong instinct to run away when they are scared. If you get one wolf on the run, it can start a chain reaction of panic. The rest of the wolves should follow.

ANTARCTICA

Human ice pops are formed at -26°F (-3°C)—the temperature at which your blood freezes! In Antarctica, the temperature can sink to -129°F (-89°C), so, yeah, not many folks choose to live there. Four thousand scientists and workers visit this c-c-coldest place on Earth in the "summer," when temperatures average a balmy -6°F (-21°C), with only one thousand staying on for the winter. They probably huddle around freezers to keep warm!

Polar Opposite

Antarctica is the coldest, windiest, and driest place on earth—not a good combo. It's so dry that it's actually considered a desert. It gets less rain and snowfall than the Sahara desert. Antarctica is a land mass covered in ice that is 2½ miles (4 km) thick in some parts. It has mountains, valleys, frozen lakes, and four active volcanos. It also has the highest average elevation of any continent. Survival in Antarctica combines Arctic (p. 20), mountain (p. 88), and desert (p. 44) endurance all in one mean package.

> **FAST FACT** • Katabatic winds are strong winds that flow down mountains and glaciers. They are a common occurrence on Antarctica and can reach strengths up to 200 miles (322 km) per hour. That's as fast as a single-engine airplane.

Penguin Party

Humans aren't the only ones who have a difficult time surviving in Antarctica. When it comes to animals on this frozen tundra, penguins pretty much have the run of the place. You can also find seals, whales, fish, and seabirds along the coast, but penguins are the only animals that dare venture inland. Emperor penguins travel up to 75 miles (125 km) inland in order to find a mate.

Early Antarctic Adventures

In the early 1900s, several countries put together teams designed to explore the un-explored continent. The first expedition to reach the South Pole was a team of five people in 1911. It took them 99 days, traveling by dog sled. They started out with fifty-two dogs and rode home with only eleven. You don't want to know what they ate!

HOW TO SURVIVE THE COLD

1 **Love the layers.** The key to staying warm is to wear layers. You'll want a foundation layer (moisture-wicking fabrics only; no cotton undies!), an insulating layer, and a windproof layer. Water-proofing isn't very important because Antarctica is so dry.

2 **Protect ears, nose, fingers, toes.** Pay careful attention to protecting your body's extremities. Don't let *anything* show, including your face and eyes. In Antarctica, exposed skin will quickly fall victim to frostbite, windburn, and sunburn.

3 **Drink up.** Cold, dry air dehydrates your body with every breath you take. It can also suck moisture right out of exposed skin. (Ever had chapped lips?) So drink a lot of fluids—including, of course, hot cocoa!

Glaciers form when snow builds up faster than it can melt—over time, the new snow compresses the fallen snow into ice. More than 98% of Antarctica is covered by glacial ice.

ARCTIC

Looking for an X-treme vacation? If you head to the Arctic, the icy region north of the Arctic Circle, you can run with the polar bears as you try to outrun frostbite! Winter temperatures can drop to -58°F (-50°C), and summer temps average about 50°F (10°C). Swimming, anyone?

Cool Customers

The Arctic is home to lots of inhabitants who know how to survive in its frigid climate. Native peoples, including the Inuit, Aleut, and Saami, have lived there for thousands of years. Plenty of animals live in the Arctic, too, including walrus, wolverines, whales, muskox, seals, caribou, and at the top of the Arctic food chain, polar bears!

Polar Predators

Polar bears are the world's largest land carnivores, standing as tall as 12 feet (3.6 m) and weighing up to 1,600 pounds (725 kg). These endangered bears, whose diet is mostly seals, eat 4½ pounds (2 kg) of fat every day to insulate their bodies from the cold. That's like drinking three large glasses of pure bacon grease daily!

FAST FACT

Polar bears live mostly above the Arctic circle, and their preferred habitat is near water, so they can hunt seals. Polar bear populations are found in Canada, the USA (Alaska), Greenland, Russia, and Norway.

Unpredictable Pole

The North Pole itself is actually frozen seawater called "polar ice pack." You can't mark the position of the North Pole for very long since the ice tends to shift around. Early Arctic explorers thought that they could reach the North Pole by ship if they waited for the right time of year…except the area is frozen all year long. Several of these attempts ended in unfortunate iceberg accidents.

How Do You Like Your Eggs?

If you have to forage for food, eggs have been a favorite snack among Arctic explorers. There are no trees, so birds lay their eggs on the ground. In the summer months, there is some plant life and some of it is edible, including Arctic raspberries and blueberries. (Smoothie, anyone?) In the coastal areas, there are hundreds of species of fish native to the Arctic Ocean, including cod, trout, and salmon. Hope you like a seafood smorgasbord!

HOW TO SURVIVE A POLAR BEAR ATTACK

1 **Keep your distance.** Yes, polar bears have been known to stalk humans. If you come face-to-face with a polar bear, you don't stand much of a chance. Your best bet is to avoid them. Try not to let them see or even smell you. If you spot one, stay downwind from it!

2 **Be a bigger bear.** If a bear starts to charge, make noise, wave your arms around, and try to appear bigger than you are. If you are with a group of people, huddle together and hold a jacket over all of your heads. Make that bear think twice about attacking.

3 **Play alive.** If all else fails, stand your ground and fight back. Kick the bear as hard as you can, quickly and repeatedly. You can only hope the bear will think you're too much trouble and give up!

4 **Back it up.** If you see a polar bear and you think it sees you, slowly back away from it without turning your back. Whatever your brain might be telling you, don't run. You won't win that race.

ASTEROIDS

You may think a killer asteroid only exists in movies and video games. But when one's about to collide with Earth—which *has* happened before!—that "fire" button on your controller won't be much help. Fortunately, like good gamers, scientists are keeping their eyes on their screens and watching for incoming rocks.

Eyeing the Asteroids

The good news is that if an asteroid is heading straight for Earth, you will probably know about it years before it hits. Space agencies, including NASA and the European Space Agency, are working on methods to crash a spacecraft directly into an asteroid and nudge it off course. The *Don Quijote* mission proposes to do just that.

Be Prepared

If the efforts to deflect the asteroid fail, look out! An asteroid crashing into the ocean would cause a giant tsunami (p. 126). Get as far away from the coast as possible. Highly populated areas are likely to be overrun with mobs (p. 82), so head for a remote, rural area, far away from the impact zone. Gather as much food, water, and medicine as possible.

Global Consequences

The aftermath of an impact event would not be pretty. A large asteroid would create a giant cloud of debris that blocked out the sun. Temperatures would drop. In time, all plant life would die. The shockwaves might cause earthquakes (p. 46) and volcanic eruptions (p. 130). Wildfires would likely break out. Basically, this is the *worst* of worst-case scenarios. Ideally, you could ride out the "impact winter" somewhere underground with large stockpiles of food and water, but let's hope it won't be necessary.

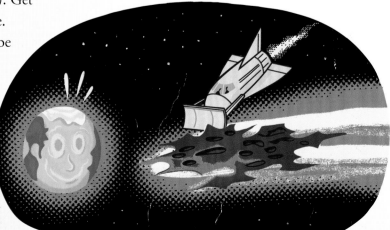

The Meteor Crater, near Flagstaff, Arizona, in the United States, is a mile (1.6km) wide.

Most asteroids are made of rock. They can be as small as a boulder or as large as hundreds of miles in diameter.

AVALANCHES

Flying down a mountain at 80 miles (129 km) per hour sounds pretty cool, doesn't it? It probably is...unless you find yourself at the front of a fast-moving avalanche. An avalanche is a huge hazard to skiers and mountain climbers. It doesn't stop for anything in its way—including you, if you're not careful!

Look Out Below!

When snow falls on a mountainside, it gets packed down over time. Then, as fresh snow falls, it creates a new layer. An avalanche begins when a slab of snow slides off the layer beneath it and moves quickly down the mountain. When the snow finally comes to a stop, it's as hard as concrete, making it extra difficult to escape from if you are buried.

Snowslide Starters

Wind, snowmobiles, and earthquakes can trigger an avalanche, as well as stepping on unstable snow. One myth is that shouting can cause them. The truth is that the sound waves from a human voice aren't strong enough to start an avalanche. Even a plane flying by is unlikely to do any damage. So feel free to *yodel-lay-hee-hoo* on snowy slopes.

FAST FACT • Ski patrol and search-and-rescue teams actually cause avalanches on purpose. They set off explosives on mountainsides to start avalanches before something, or someone, else does.

Beacon of Hope

If you are hiking in snowy mountains, especially in remote areas called backcountry, everyone in your group should carry an avalanche beacon. If you get buried, these radio devices send out signals by making a beeping sound, letting your buddies above ground know where you are. If you have two beacons, you can practice using them at home—like playing a high-tech game of hide-and-seek.

HOW TO SURVIVE AN AVALANCHE

1 **Ditch it.** Backpacks, skis, and ski poles will only weigh you down. Drop everything if an avalanche is speeding toward you.

2 **Move on up.** If you start an avalanche by walking on unstable snow, act fast! Get yourself uphill from the slide before it takes you for a ride.

3 **Be a tree hugger.** If you can't get out of the way of the slide, hold on to a tree for dear life!

4 **Snow swim.** If the slide sweeps you up, try using the front crawl to get yourself near the surface.

5 **Form a pocket.** If you feel yourself getting buried, cup a hand around your mouth to form an air pocket in the snow. Also, try to stick one of your limbs through the snow so rescuers can locate you easily.

BEARS

Thanks to the cuddly, stuffed teddy, you probably have a warm and fuzzy feeling about bears. But a bear in the flesh is about as huggable às a running chainsaw. Encountering a black bear or brown bear can be scary, to say the least. Here are the bear essentials.

Bamboo Panda

Bears are omnivores that eat a combination of meat and plants, but the giant panda is an exception. The panda's diet is 99 percent bamboo. It eats 20 to 40 pounds (9 to 18 kg) of bamboo each day. That's like a human eating 160 hamburgers! Munching bamboo is a full-time job for the panda. A panda spends up to ten hours a day stuffing its face.

Two grizzly bears wrestling in Katmai National Park, Alaska, United States.

In the wild, giant pandas are found exclusively in the mountains of central China where, scientists estimate, about 1600 are left.

Bigger Bear

The polar bear claims this title, but the Kodiak bear, the largest of the brown bears, is a close second. Also called Alaskan grizzlies—they live only on the Kodiak Archipelago, a group of islands off the coast of Alaska in the United States—these "scare" bears have been isolated from other bears for more than 12,000 years. Kodiak bears can grow up to 10 feet (3 m) long and weigh as much as 1,500 pounds (680 kg).

Brand New Bear?

Discoveries in 2006 and 2010 show that polar bears and grizzlies are mating and making a whole new type of bear, informally known as a "pizzly bear," or a "grolar bear." This rare hybrid has light fur like a polar bear, with brown paws and a grizzly-like head.

HOW TO CAMP BEAR-FREE

1 Look for signs. If you are camping in a designated camp-site, park rangers will post signs that warn of recent bear activity. If possible, move to a different campsite that is bear-free.

2 Play keep away. Odors attract bears to campsites. So store all food, food equipment, toiletries, and garbage away from your site. Good storage places include bear-proof containers, a car trunk, a boat anchored offshore, or a tree—hang items 4 feet (1 m) from a tree branch that is at least 14 feet (4 m) high.

3 Change your clothes. Even your clothes can collect food odors. Change into clean clothing and store your dirty duds with the items in step 2 before hitting the sack.

4 Make some noise. If a bear still insists on visiting your camp-site, bang pots and pans together and throw rocks and sticks to scare it away. If the bear doesn't retreat, you should. Once in a safe place, report the bear sighting to a park ranger.

BEES

We swat, shriek, and run when we hear that dreaded buzz. But is that any way to greet the world's greatest honey producer, wax and medicine maker, and all-important flower pollinator? The bee gets a bad rap because of its pointy bee-hind, but if you are aware of some ABeeCs, you can avoid getting stung.

Bee Aware

A bee sting can be more than just a pain in the butt. Some people have severe allergies to stings. In the United States, bee stings actually kill three times as many people a year as snakebites! Almost everyone has some kind of allergic reaction to bees, which is why a sting swells up. Luckily, less than 1 percent of the population has the deadly allergy.

Honeybees swarm together to start a new colony.

If a bee lands on you, stay still until it flies away.

Killer Bees

Killer bees are a hybrid of African and European honeybees. They started out in South America about fifty years ago and are steadily moving north. They are more aggressive and more likely to attack as a group—and will chase you farther—than other bees. These bad news bees can kill a person who isn't even allergic. If you are attacked by killer bees, you should run. Get inside as soon as possible and close all windows and doors. If you can't reach shelter, run through bushes or high weeds to keep you covered.

Where Could They Bee?

In 2006, beekeepers began to notice that worker bees were abandoning the hive and leaving the queen all by herself. Scientists call this "Colony Collapse Disorder." No one is exactly sure what causes it. Some theories involve pesticides, viruses, a fungus, or all of the above. If bees do become extinct, the world will have a shortage of food. No pollination means no crops!

HOW TO AVOID A BEE STING

1. **None of your beeswax.** If you find a beehive, keep your distance. Bees are defensive. One bee sting might not be a big deal, but hundreds of bees swarming around you is a whole different story.

2. **Turn off flower power.** You don't want to look and smell like a giant flower. Avoid wearing flowery perfumes, soaps, or lotions. Also, don't wear brightly colored clothing.

3. **Bee calm.** If a bee lands on you, don't move until it flies away. If you flail your arms and run around, you are more likely to get stung.

4. **Buzz off.** If you do get stung, scrape the stinger out of your body with a fingernail. Don't pinch or squeeze the stinger, which could just release more venom into your body.

BERMUDA TRIANGLE

You've probably experienced a dead zone: that annoying spot in your home where cell-phone calls are mysteriously dropped. Well, the Bermuda Triangle is the original dead zone...except some ships and planes have mysteriously "dropped" when they traveled through it. Since there's no explanation for this phenomenon, it's best to steer clear of these weird waters!

Which Way Is North?

The most often reported mystery in the Bermuda Triangle is that compasses don't work correctly. One known case of a compass malfunction occurred on December 5, 1945. Flight 19, also known as "The Lost Patrol," was a team of five bombers that flew through the Bermuda Triangle. The flight leader reported to controllers that his two compasses were not working. The planes became hopelessly lost and eventually ran out of fuel. Wreckage was never found.

Differing Views

A few of the more outlandish theories about the Bermuda Triangle say that strange magnetic fields are at work. Triangle-believers think that it is an intergalactic space portal, a time warp, or a door to another dimension. Skeptics point to pirates (*argh!*), human error (*oops!*), and strong ocean currents (*whoosh!*).

FAST FACT • Lloyd's of London began its business more than 300 years ago as insurers of ships and cargo. Their maritime records show that the number of tragedies in the Bermuda Triangle is similar to losses in other parts of the world. Could the Bermuda Triangle just be a myth?

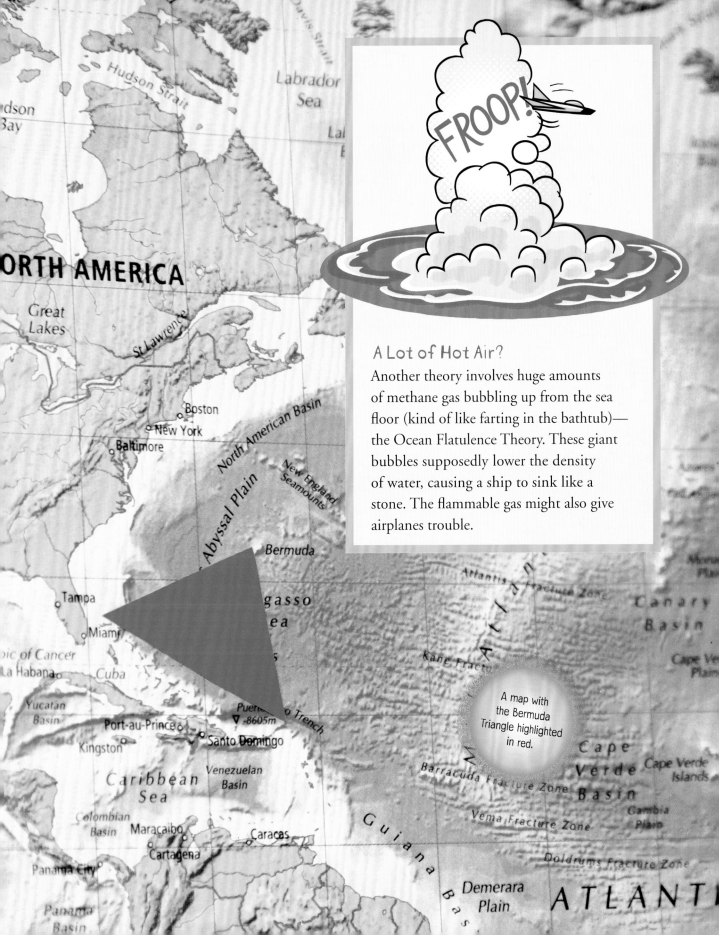

FROOP!

A Lot of Hot Air?

Another theory involves huge amounts of methane gas bubbling up from the sea floor (kind of like farting in the bathtub)— the Ocean Flatulence Theory. These giant bubbles supposedly lower the density of water, causing a ship to sink like a stone. The flammable gas might also give airplanes trouble.

A map with the Bermuda Triangle highlighted in red.

BLIZZARDS

Imagine standing in a snow globe that's being shaken by a demented giant. That's pretty much what it feels like to be caught in a blustery blizzard. A blizzard is like the hurricane of snow. Winds must reach 35 miles (56 km) per hour to classify a storm as a blizzard. That's one powerful snowstorm!

Expect the Unexpected

Blizzards can be most dangerous in places where they are least expected. A 1972 blizzard in Iran—the deadliest on record—may have brought an end to a four-year drought, but it buried entire villages and caused over four thousand deaths.

Whiteout!

A whiteout is exactly what it sounds like: you can't see anything but white. Riding in a car when a blizzard strikes is one of the most dangerous places to be. In February 2001, a 117-car pileup occurred on an interstate in Virginia in the United States during a whiteout, killing one person and injuring thirty-one others. If you know a blizzard is on the way, stay off the roads.

Brrr!

Even if you're at home during a blizzard, it may not be so cozy. The power can go out, and because most people depend on electricity for heat, you could be in for a chilly time. Wrap yourself in a thick blanket (or two or three) to keep warm until power is restored. If you use an alternative heating source, like a fireplace or kerosene heater, follow local fire department guidelines. Make sure your flashlights have fresh batteries and keep bottled water and nonperishable food items on hand.

Blizzards lead to very dangerous driving conditions, especially on highways.

HOW TO RIDE OUT A BLIZZARD IN A CAR

1 **Stay put.** Unless you can actually see safe shelter up ahead, stick with the car. It is easy to get disoriented in whiteout conditions. No one should attempt to go for help until the storm is over.

2 **Ten on, fifty off.** Your mom or dad should run the engine with the heat on for 10 minutes every hour. Doing this will help save gas and keep deadly fumes from building up in the car. Crack a window from time to time for fresh air.

3 **Keep active.** Move around to keep your blood flowing and your body temperature up. Clap your hands, arm wrestle, or sing some tunes. Someone should be awake at all times in case a rescue crew passes by.

4 **Snow signal.** If you need a rescue after the storm, stomp an "X" or the word "HELP" in the snow next to your car. Make it big! Waving a bright piece of clothing will also attract attention.

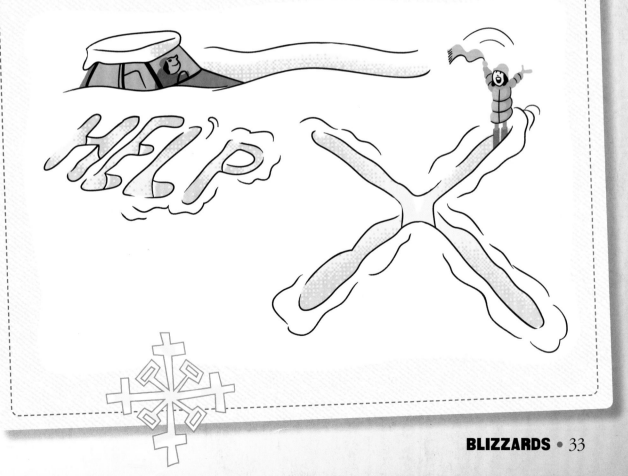

BULL RUNNING

You're the fastest sprinter in your school. You love the competitive thrill of overtaking the other racers. But can you outrun a bull? Every July 6 to 14, thousands of people risk life, limb, and bottom to run with the bulls in the streets of Pamplona, Spain, in celebration of the Festival of San Fermin. Here's how to come back from the bull run intact.

Rise and Shine

How'd you like to wake up to find a bull staring at you? The bull runs take place at eight in the morning. A dozen bulls are released from their pens so they can run to the bullring. Runners dress in all white with red sashes and scarves. Fireworks are set off to signal that the bulls have been released from the corral, and to alert the runners that the bulls have started running into town. This is when most people run for cover!

Here They Come!

As the bulls charge into town, snorting, huffing, and ready to gore anything in their path, the (human) runners start hoofing it, too. The objective of people who run with the

BE AWARE • There are four rockets that go off during the event, and they have very significant meanings for runners. First rocket: The corral gates have been opened for the bulls. And you should start running! Second rocket: All six of the bulls are out of their pens and running. Third rocket: The bulls have reached the bullring, but you're not out of the danger zone yet. Fourth rocket: The bulls are in their pens. You can stop running now!

Runners get out of the way of charging bulls at the Festival of San Fermin in Pamplona, Spain.

bulls in Pamplona is to stay as close to them as possible without getting hurt. The route is a little more than a ½ mile (825 meters) over narrow, cobbled streets. It takes only a few minutes to complete the race to the bullfighting arena—but they may feel like the longest minutes of your life! *Olé!*

Raging Bulls

It shouldn't be a surprise that running with the bulls in Pamplona is as dangerous as it looks. Every year, dozens of runners get injured, often seriously. Most get hurt after falling, but some are gored and trampled by the big beasts. Since 1924, fifteen people have been killed.

HOW TO SURVIVE RUNNING WITH THE BULLS

1 **Know before you go.** Walk the course the day before so the twists and turns won't confuse you. You want to run away from the bulls, not into them.

2 **Plan your escape.** Look for doorways you can press yourself into, places where you can climb the fence, or gaps in the fence you can fit through. Keep in mind that other runners may try to escape the same way.

3 **Tight turns.** The bulls tend to take corners on the outside, so the smart runners stick to the inside.

4 **If you go down, stay down.** Many people are injured when they trip (often over others who have fallen) and then jump back up—into the path of an oncoming bull. The safest thing to do is stay down, cover your head, and wait. Traditionally, a spectator will tap you on the shoulder when all is clear.

BUNGEE JUMPING

If all your friends were jumping off a bridge, would you do it, too? The excitement of bungee jumping, a harnessed method of diving, is all about the feel of the fall and the jolt of the bounce on your way back up. But if you're thinking of taking the plunge, look out (and read on) below!

Di-vine Inspiration

Vine jumping, also known as land diving, inspired modern-day bungee jumping. Native people from the island of Pentecost in the South Pacific invented this practice centuries ago. Every year, men from the island climb wooden platforms up to 100 feet (30.5 m) high. They tie a vine to each ankle and take the plunge. The goal is to just barely touch the ground. Yikes!

Bungee Beginnings

The members of the Dangerous Sports Club (who else?) in England were the first to use actual bungee cords. A bungee cord is basically a bunch of elastic bands wrapped

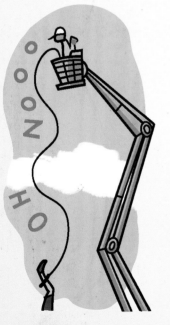

CRANE JUMP

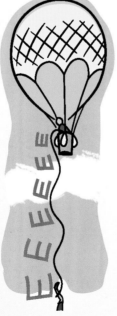

HOT AIR BALLOON JUMP

BRIDGE JUMP

You can bungee jump from bridges, dams, cable cars, platforms jutting from skyscrapers, cranes, and even hot air balloons. Here are some of the tallest venues to fall from around the world.

Royal Gorge Bridge *Colorado, United States.* The highest suspension bridge in the United States, it spans the Grand Canyon and is a whopping 1,053 feet (321 m) high.

Macau Tower *Macau, China.* This building stands at 1,092 feet (333 m) and has a bungee-jump platform as part of its "Skywalk" 764 feet (233 m) up.

Verzasca Dam *Ticino, Switzerland.* Dams are popular venues for bungee jumps, but none stand as high as this one at 721 feet (220 m).

Nevis Highwire *Queenstown, New Zealand.* If the thought of being supported 440 feet (134 m) in the air by a couple of cables doesn't scare you, this cable-car jump is for you.

in nylon. This club watched a film about the vine jumpers in the South Pacific and decided the activity needed an upgrade. On April Fools' Day in 1979, they bungee jumped off a suspension bridge in Bristol, England. The police arrested the adventurers but that didn't stop them. The extreme sport of bungee jumping was born.

Oh, Snap!

It should come as no surprise that bungee jumping can be dangerous. Bungee cords do snap from time to time. A more common problem is a too-long cord. A bungee cord can stretch out over time. Another concern is getting tangled up in the cord. Still think you've got what it takes? Choose a bungee jumping biz with a good safety record!

A bungee jump high above a river gorge.

CLIMBING

"Murder Wall," "Killer Mountain," and "Man Eater" sound like the prison names of super-scary criminals. They're actually nicknames given to the world's biggest, baddest mountains. When scaling a mountain, a *lot* can go wrong. But if you're shooting to touch the sky and come back to tell the (tall) tale, read on.

Top of the World

Even for an elite mountaineer, to conquer one of the world's massive peaks takes years of training. Altitude is a tough foe; lack of oxygen is deadly. Only 153 people have ever made it to the top of Annapurna, in central Nepal, and 58 have died trying—that's a death rate of nearly 40 percent! At more than 26,000 feet (8,000 m), it is NOT recommended for weekend hikers.

Snow Trouble

When climbers first ascended Mont Blanc in the French Alps in 1786, it was an amazing feat. These days, about 20,000 people make it to the summit each year—though at least 50 people died on this mountain in 2008 alone. Mont Blanc is far from tame, and its popularity may have made it even more dangerous—more climbers increase the risk of an avalanche (p. 24).

Day Trippers...and Fallers

Mount Washington in New Hampshire is the tallest mountain in the eastern United States. It stands "only" 6,288 feet (1,917 m) above sea level, and experienced trekkers can climb it in a day. But do not underestimate this mountain. Since 1849, at least 140 people have died on its slopes, many from hypothermia. The weather station on the summit is called the "Home of the World's Worst Weather," with temperatures as low as -47ºF (-43ºC) and wind speeds of up to 231 miles (371 km) per hour. Not a good place to plan a picnic!

Mountaineers climbing Mt. Everest, the tallest mountain in the world. It stands at 29,035 feet (8,850 m).

FAST FACT • Famous mountaineer Reinhold Messner was the first to summit all fourteen of the eight-thousanders. It took him sixteen years. He completed this feat in 1986.

A climber tackling an ice wall.

CORAL REEFS

A coral reef is like an underwater city: it's colorful, full of diversity, and can be particularly dangerous for visitors! People love exploring reefs, which are the rain forests of the sea. But before you go poking around in one of these watery ecosystems, be aware of what's lurking just beneath the surface.

Pretty Shell? Not So Fast...

Visitors to coral reefs love to comb the beaches and reefs for seashells. But not everything on the sea floor is safe to pick up. You might not think of a sea snail as deadly, but the cone snail packs a fatal punch. Its colorful shell hides a venomous harpoon that the snail uses to spear its victims. Of the five hundred varieties of this snail—all of them venomous—most will only give you a bee-like sting. But the larger snails, like the geographic cone snail, are responsible for at least thirty human deaths over the last 300 years.

Don't Tread on Me

The stonefish—found in the Great Barrier Reef off the coast of Australia—is the most venomous fish in the world. It looks just like an encrusted stone (hence, it's name), making it easy to step on accidentally. The stonefish's dorsal fin is lined with thirteen needle-like stingers, and its sting is one of the most painful experiences—victims say it feels like getting smashed in the foot with a sledge-hammer. It can be lethal without treatment. Divers aren't the only ones who need to be wary of this nasty little fish. The stonefish can survive up to twenty hours outside of the water, so beach walkers beware.

CORAL KILLERS

Stonefish. Each of the stonefish's thirteen needlelike stingers has enough venom to kill approximately 1,000 mice.

Blue Ringed Octopus. Though it's only the size of a tennis ball, it carries enough venom to kill up to twenty-six people! One sting from this octopus can cause a person to go blind in seconds.

Lionfish. This colorful little fish is lined with spikes, kind of like a porcupine. And if you prick yourself on one of these spikes, you're in big trouble. This little guy is almost as venomous as the stonefish.

Sea Snake. Though more venomous than its counterpart on land, this serpent is shy and very rarely bites... unless provoked.

DESERTED ISLANDS

It may sound fun at first: a tropical paradise all to yourself! But if you're stranded on a deserted island, no one's there to cook you dinner, either. You'll need to find food and prepare for just about everything else, too. If you're stranded, here's how to survive and thrive.

It's Your Island Now

Look on the bright side: people pay millions of dollars for private islands—you landed on yours for free! Explore your new home and see what it has to offer. Note places where you can fetch freshwater and food, like coconuts (they have lots of vitamin C, calcium, potassium, and fiber) and mangoes (they are high in vitamins A and C and fiber).

Solar Power

Finding water is your top priority. If you can't find freshwater inland, you'll have to get creative. Since you can't always rely on the weather for rain, tie fabric around your ankles and walk through grass or foliage to collect dew, then wring out the water into a vessel. If you don't have an obvious container, a tarp, stretched fabric, a hollowed-out coconut, or even a life raft will work.

SOS

Now that you've made yourself at home, you can focus on being rescued. Make a distress signal out of seaweed, rocks, palm leaves, or anything that stands out against the beach. Your signal should be in a prominent spot, and big enough so that it can be read from the air. The universal distress signal is three triangles in a row.

HOW TO OPEN A COCONUT

1. **Find a stick.** Find a long stick that comes up to about your waist.

2. **Carve it to a point.** Sharpen one end of the stick so that it comes to a nice point. If you don't have a pocket knife, you can rub the end of the stick at an angle against a rock. Stick the other end of the stick firmly into the ground.

3. **Bash it.** Using both hands (and all of your strength), crack the outer shell: raise the coconut over your head, then bash it on the sharp point of the stick.

4. **Smash it.** The inner shell of the coconut is easier to open. Throw it against a rock or tree to get to the meat of it.

FAST FACT • A real-life castaway inspired the novel *Robinson Crusoe* by Daniel Defoe. Alexander Selkirk was marooned on an island in the South Pacific in 1704. He survived for 4 years before he was rescued.

This deserted island in the Caribbean looks like the ultimate vacation spot...until you're stranded there.

DESERTS

Deserts are known for their blazing temperatures, but it's not the hot-hot heat that makes a desert, well, a desert. It's the lack of rainfall. A desert is a region that gets less than 10 inches (25 cm) of rain a year. Most plants need far more water to survive, turning water into a virtual dessert for a desert plant.

Beat the Heat

After a few hours in the desert sun, you might be tempted to strip off your clothes to cool down. But stay covered up. Clothing not only protects you from the sun, it also holds your sweat longer, helping to cool your body. If you find a rare shady spot, rest there and travel at dusk.

Get Some Perspective

If you are lost in the desert, head for the highest point to get the best view. You might spot a road, some power lines, or even a town off in the distance. Travel along a ridge to make it easier for you to spot rescuers, and for rescuers to spot you.

Desert Driving

Cars often break down in desert conditions. Don't abandon your car. It provides valuable shelter and is easier to spot than a person. Bring lots of water when traveling through the desert—3 gallons (11 L) per person should be enough for three days. You might want to bring 6 gallons (22 L) just to be on the safe side.

SHINE ON

Reflecting light with a mirror can make a great distress signal. The barren landscape and sunny skies of the desert make it possible for this little glint of light to be seen miles away. A wristwatch, compass, aluminum can, piece of foil, or pair of glasses, can be used the same way.

A portion of the Sahara desert in Libya. The Sahara is 3.5 million square miles (8.6 km²), or one-third of Africa.

HOW TO FIND WATER IN THE DESERT

1 **Dig in.** If you are dying of thirst, a dry stream might look like a cruel joke, but don't despair—dig! Look for wet sand at the outer edge of a sharp bend in the dry creek bed, then dig 3 to 6 feet (0.9 to 1.8 meters). Water flows downhill so check out the base of rocky cliffs where water often collects. Look for damp soil and dig.

2 **Just dew it.** Even in the desert, dew forms on plants in the mornings. Scrape this precious moisture into your mouth. Every drop counts!

3 **Track it down.** Animals need water, too. If you follow animal tracks, they may lead to an oasis. Birds or bird poop are also clues that water might be nearby.

4 **Chew on this.** Cut open the stalk of a cactus and chew on the pith (don't swallow it). The pith will help alleviate thirst.

EARTHQUAKES

If you start feeling a shake, rattle, and roll, and you're not on a dance floor, you may be experiencing an earthquake. Quakes can feel either like a light vibration or a violent rumbling that shakes you (and your house) to the foundation. An earthquake may start deep in the ground, but it can have major effects on everything up above.

On Shaky Ground

Believe it or not, *thousands* of earthquakes happen every day. Most are too small to even be noticed because Earth's surface is actually cracked and split into large sections called tectonic plates. The plates shift every day, but not very fast. The fastest-moving plate only travels about 6 inches (15 cm) in a year. At that pace, it would take you eighty years to walk the length of a school bus!

Colossal Collisions

What tectonic plates lack in speed, they make up for with sheer power. When two tectonic plates bump into each other, they can form entire mountain ranges…in super slow motion over millions of years. In fact, just 250 million years ago, all of the continents may have been connected in one giant land mass called Pangaea. According to this theory, the movement of tectonic plates broke Pangaea apart and gave shape to the world we know today.

Damage to a school in the Sichuan Province of China from a 7.9-magnitude earthquake that hit on May 12, 2008, and killed 70,000 people.

Blame it on the Fault

Earthquakes can happen anywhere, but they are most likely to occur along fault lines. Fault lines mark the boundaries between tectonic plates and routinely push and shove against each other. The San Andreas Fault runs through California in the United States, causing thousands of earthquakes (most too small to be felt) each year. In 1906, a rupture on the San Andreas Fault all but destroyed the city of San Francisco. Over 28,000 buildings were lost in the earthquake and the fires that followed it.

HOW TO SURVIVE AN EARTHQUAKE

2 **Open up.** If you are outside during an earthquake, get to an open area as soon as possible. Steer clear of power lines, buildings, bridges, and anything else that might fall on you.

1 **Go under cover.** If you are indoors, seek cover under a desk or a table, and hang on! Crouching under a doorway will also give you some protection. And stay away from the kitchen! Kitchens often have gas lines that can rupture during a quake and cause an explosive fire.

3 **Quake in your boots.** After the quake, put on some boots or thick-soled shoes. You might have to walk on broken glass and other dangerous debris. Also be prepared for aftershocks, smaller earthquakes that follow the main quake.

BE AWARE • Being in the mountains doesn't mean you're safe from a quake. In mountainous terrain, earthquakes can trigger falling rocks (p. 54), avalanches (p. 24), and mudslides (p. 90).

ELECTRIC EELS

It's shocking—positively shocking!—how dangerous the electric eel can be. An underwater creature that lives in the Amazon River basin in South America, these 6-foot-long (1.8-m) electric fish emit up to 150 high-powered shocks an hour. That's more than two a minute. Ouch!

Top of the Food Chain

Electric eels are apex predators—they have nothing to fear from any other animal because they are at the top of the food chain. Anything that tries to attack this eel is in for a shocking surprise. The electric eel can deliver a 600-volt jolt of electricity that is five times as many volts as a standard wall socket.

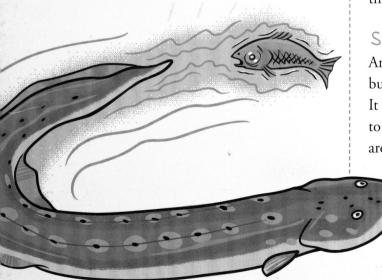

Simply Shocking

Electric eels don't just use their secret weapon for defense, they also use electricity to track and capture prey. Electric eels have very poor eyesight, so while they hunt, they send out little zaps of around 10 volts, which act like a radar system. When electric eels locate prey, they dial up the juice to stun their victim, then swallow it whole.

Shock Me Once...

An electric eel can give you a nasty shock, but it's not very likely for it to kill a human. It would take several shocks, or multiple eels, to bring you down. But if you are wading around in the Amazon River (not a good idea to begin with), watch your step. If you feel a shock, get out of the water immediately. You don't want to find out how many shocks it actually takes.

FAST FACT
The electric eel needs air to survive. If it doesn't surface every few minutes to get some oxygen, it will die.

An electric eel is more closely related to a catfish than an eel. Can you see the resemblance?

ELECTRICITY

You come home, flip on the lights, grab something from the fridge, then turn on your computer. Could you get through a day without electricity and the ridiculously useful things it does for you? It would be tough. But those strong currents can also do some powerful damage. It's time to shed some light on the dark side of electricity.

All Aboard!

Something that transmits electricity or heat easily is called a conductor. Most metals are great conductors. Water is a good one, too. The human body is around 60 percent water, which means *you* are a good conductor. Never touch live wires, sockets, or plugs in a socket. And don't stick a fork into the toaster, or you'll be the one cooking.

Down to Earth

Electricity always wants to reach the ground and will take shortcuts to get there. You don't want to be that shortcut. So don't fly a kite near power lines. Also, don't pull a Ben Franklin and fly a kite during a thunderstorm. In 1753, a Russian physicist tried to recreate the famous kite experiment and died by electrocution.

Calm After the Storm?

After a storm has passed through your area, be aware of downed power lines. Even if the lines are not sparking, they are still extremely dangerous. Storms usually leave a lot of water behind, and downed lines can electrify puddles of water and even wet trees.

Car Trouble

If a power line falls on the car you're riding in, call for help and stay put. But if your car catches fire, you will have to jump for it. Try not to touch the outside of the car. And never touch the car and the ground at the same time. Remember, electricity wants to reach the ground, and it has no qualms about using your body to get there.

FAST FACT • Ben Franklin believed that electrocuting turkeys made the meat tender. In 1750, while preparing to zap a Christmas turkey, he ended up giving himself a nearly lethal shock. There's got to be a better way!

DON'T BECOME A CONDUCTOR

The right way to rescue toast: unplug the toaster and flip it over. Shake gently to release toast.

WRONG

RIGHT

The Tesla coil, invented by Nikola Tesla in 1891, produces high voltage. The voltage here is close to 100 kilovolts.

ELEVATORS

Imagine walking up eighty flights of stairs to a friend's apartment, then realizing you've forgotten what you meant to bring! Thank goodness for the invention of the elevator. This amazing contraption can occasionally malfunction, alas. Here's what to do if yours goes haywire and you need to become an elevator operator on the spot.

Patience, Please

Most elevator accidents happen when people are in a rush and abuse the safety features. For example, elevator doors have sensors that detect something in the way. People often stick an arm or a leg in between the doors, knowing they will pop back open. But you can never be sure that these safety features are working. By the time you find out, it could be too late. Best bet: keep your body parts away from the door!

Going Up!

The biggest fear people have about elevators is that the cable will snap and the elevator will plummet. What most people don't know is that an elevator can also "fall" up! A counterweight is attached to an elevator to help it rise through the building. If something goes wrong, this counterweight can send an elevator soaring upwards as fast as 60 miles (96 km) per hour!

Glass elevators in a hotel.

Sticky Situation

Getting stuck in an elevator is pretty common. If it happens to you, don't try to escape through the service hatch—the elevator could start moving again at any second. Play the waiting game instead. Use the intercom to call for help. Flick the emergency switch to sound the alarm. A cell phone can also be useful to call for help, or to cure boredom. And don't panic! It's a myth that an elevator will eventually run out of air. There's plenty of air circulating in the elevator shaft.

PROTECT
YOURSELF

LIE
FLAT

HOW TO SURVIVE A PLUMMETING ELEVATOR

1 **Don't jump.** Some people think that if they jump at just the right moment, they will float to safety. Don't fall into that trap: the elevator car could collapse on impact. If you time your jump perfectly you'll only succeed in smashing into the ceiling first, then crashing to the ground.

2 **Flatten out.** Your best chance of survival is to lie flat on the floor in the center of the elevator. Doing this will distribute the force of impact evenly.

3 **Cover up.** Cover your face and head to help protect you from ceiling parts that may break loose.

FALLING ROCK

"Rock on!" means good times are on the horizon. "Falling rock!" means your horizon is about to smash. Getting rained on by rocks can lead to serious injury. So if you're hiking a trail or riding in a car in mountainous terrain and rocks start tumbling, that's your cue to exit rock-star style.

Rock and Roll

When traveling by car, you most often see falling rock signs in the mountains. Areas with harsh winters or lots of rain usually have the loosest rock. When rock falls into the road, there's not much you can do except drive around it. (And get off that road!)

Ups and Downs

Wherever there are rocky surfaces, you can be pretty confident that rocks will eventually fall. Before you climb a mountain or cliff, look for signs of recent tumbles, such as holes or strange formations where erosion has taken its toll.

Rock Opera

When climbing, always wear a helmet. One of the most important rules to follow is never climb below other groups. People climbing above you may free up loose rocks and send them tumbling down. If you happen to be the one who sends the rocks tumbling down, let others know. What should you yell? "Rock!"

Rockfalls are a common threat along scenic Chapman's Peak Drive near Cape Town, South Africa.

HOW TO FREE YOURSELF FROM FALLEN ROCK

1 **Dig in.** If you are trapped under a rock and can move, dig at the edges of it with your hands or a stick or sharp rock. Doing this will help you shift the rock's weight. Attempt to move the rock in every direction, pushing your whole body against the rock if you can.

3 **Slip away.** You can also try greasing your trapped body part with lip balm or sunscreen to make it slippery. If you are in snow country, grab a nearby chunk of ice and try cooling the body part that's trapped to numb the pain and minimize swelling.

2 **Give it a pry.** If you can get a hold of a stout stick, insert one end of the stick under the boulder. Then lift up on the stick and try to pry the rock away from you.

4 **Keep your cool.** If you are unable to free yourself, stay calm. You need to conserve your energy. If you are alone, call out for help at regular intervals. If someone does hear your cry, they'll need to follow your voice to find you.

FLOODS

Floating down a river can be very peaceful—unless that river is where your street used to be! A flood can happen anywhere, anytime, thanks to heavy rains, big storms, or surging ocean water. If you don't own an ark, you'll need to know how to outwit the waters and stay afloat.

In a Flash

Flash floods have two deadly features: they appear with little warning, and they are the fastest-moving kind of flood. Flash floods often happen when heavy rain falls in a short amount of time, or when water barriers, like a levee or a dam, break apart.

That Time of Year

Flooding along rivers is normal and even expected. Some river floods occur seasonally, particularly in the spring when winter snow melts and combines with spring showers. Monsoons are seasonal wind and rainstorms that mostly affect southern Asia and can cause floods each year.

FAST FACT • Urban areas are not immune to flooding. When land is paved or cemented, it loses its ability to absorb water. When too much rain collects, roads turn into rivers and parking lots become ponds.

The Coast Is Cleared

Coastal flooding is usually caused by hurricanes and tropical storms. The storms push ocean water onto the land in surges. Top off a surge with oversized waves, and it's a recipe for disaster. Houses can be swept away in the blink of an eye.

A flooded road and bridge in Manitoba, Canada.

ROAD CLOSED

ROUTE BARRÉE

HOW TO SURVIVE A FLOOD

1 Heed warnings. If there is a flood watch or warning, pay attention to it. If you live in a flood zone, evacuate to higher ground.

2 Live out loud. If you are stuck in your house, move to the highest floor or even the roof. Use a cell phone to call for help. Grab a white shirt plus anything that makes noise, so you can signal to rescuers.

3 Go with the flow. Never cross floodwater! Six inches (15cm)—the amount of water that comes up to your knees—of rapidly moving floodwater can knock down an adult. If a flash flood is coming your way, run! If the water knocks you down, float on your back with your feet pointing in the direction that the water is flowing. Try to grab something that's not moving, like a tree, and climb out.

4 Drink bottled water. Flood-waters are filled with germs and toxins. So do not eat or drink anything that has been contaminated by them.

FLU PANDEMICS

Getting the flu stinks. With its aches, pains, fever, and chills, the flu makes you feel so lousy, you don't even enjoy being able to skip school. But if you can protect yourself during the germ warfare, you need not panic about this pandemic.

Mutant Viruses

There are many different kinds of flu viruses, and they change, or mutate, each year. About every ten years, the virus has a major change. That's when otherwise healthy people get deadly cases. A large-scale outbreak is called an *epidemic*. If it goes global, it's a *pandemic*.

Pandemonium

There have been four pandemics in the last one hundred years. The Spanish Flu of 1918 killed between fifty and one hundred million people in two years. It even spread to the Arctic. It was one of the deadliest natural disasters in history. The Asian Flu of 1957 and 1958 killed at least a million people. The Hong Kong Flu also killed about one million people worldwide between 1968 and 1969.

Oink! Oink!

H1N1, popularly known as the "swine flu," was first found in the United States and Mexico in April 2009. The disease spread worldwide in only six weeks and was declared a pandemic by June. Thankfully, it was not as deadly as earlier pandemics.

A microscopic view of the H1N1 flu virus.

A flu virus particle, or virion, is extremely tiny—so small that it can be seen only with an electron microscope.

HOW TO AVOID AN EPIDEMIC

1 **Wash up.** Wash your hands thoroughly and often with warm water and soap for as long as it takes to sing the ABC song (slowly).

2 **Clean up.** Regularly clean places in your home that people touch, like light switches, door handles, and phones. Empty garbage bins often (especially if snotty tissues are adding up).

3 **Lay low.** If there is a flu epidemic in your area, stay away from places where lots of people gather, like movie theaters and malls. You may even have a legitimate chance to miss some school!

4 **No pain, no gain.** Get a seasonal flu shot. If there is also a shot for a specific strain of flu, get that, too. Double ouch.

FOG

Both mysterious and plain old misty, fog makes for instant atmosphere. Unfortunately, that atmospheric pea-soup sky can lead to car crashes, boat disasters, and airplane snafus. Though it doesn't appear to be as dangerous as other severe weather events, the hazards of fog are clear as day. But with these tips, fog won't faze you.

Fog Log

There are four main kinds of fog: When the ground becomes cooled by the night sky, then cools the air above the ground—*radiation fog*. When warm air moves over a cool surface, like when ocean air blows over land—*advection fog*. When warm air passes over the slope of a cool mountain—*upslope fog*. When water vapor enters air that is already quite full of water—*evaporation fog*. How your brain feels after all that—foggy.

Wet and Wild

Fog is essentially a cloud that is touching the ground. It is filled with tiny droplets that hover very closely together and are not quite big enough to fall as rain. Fog can be so dense that light has a difficult time shining through it. If you're trying to find your way out of night fog, don't shine a bright flashlight. The droplets will reflect the light back, making it harder for you to see. Turn the lights down low to light your way.

In a Fog

You create your own fog when it is cold and you breathe into the air. That's when you see a little cloud coming from your mouth. The air coming from your mouth is warm and moist, unlike the air surrounding you. Ta-da, fog!

FAST FACT • Tule (pronounced too-lee) fog is a kind of radiation fog that occurs in parts of California in the United States. It happens during the rainy season in the late fall and winter. Tule fog makes for very low visibility and is a leading cause of weather-related deaths in California.

OPPOSITE: The south tower of the Golden Gate Bridge in San Francisco, California, United States.

FOUR KINDS OF FOG

RADIATION FOG

UPSLOPE FOG

ADVECTION FOG

EVAPORATION FOG

GORILLAS

From King Kong to Donkey Kong, these on-screen gorillas make a habit of grabbing goods and girls and scaling tall structures. But if you're face-to-face with this great ape in the real world, try these tips before this 6-foot (1.8-m), 500-pound (227-kg) primate attempts to peel you like a banana.

Where in the World?

Gorillas are found in mountain forests and lowland tropical forests in Africa. The population of mountain gorillas has fallen to as low as 700 due to human poaching, destruction of their habitats, and diseases, like the Ebola virus. Areas where these gorillas live are now protected parks. Though still considered endangered, lowland gorillas are in much better shape. There are as many as 150,000 lowland gorillas thriving today.

FAST FACT • In 1996, at the Brookfield Zoo near Chicago in the United States, a three-year-old boy fell into a gorilla exhibit. A female gorilla picked up the child, gently cradled him in her arms, and promptly delivered the boy to zookeepers at the entrance to the exhibit.

Group Hug

Gorillas live in groups of 5 to 30 apes called "troops." They are very social with one another, grooming each other and taking group walks to forage for food. Gorilla parents are very affectionate and patient with their young. A dominant silverback male leads each band of gorillas, organizing where the group eats, sleeps, and looks for food. He even settles disputes between family members. Imagine complaining to a silverback the next time your sister borrows your favorite jeans without asking!

Gorillas are actually quite shy, and they are vegetarians.

A band of eastern lowland gorillas hang around their leader in the forest.

HOW TO SURVIVE A GORILLA ENCOUNTER

1 **Do judge.** An angry gorilla will scream, beat his chest, and bare his teeth to show his rank. A playful or curious gorilla will merely grab at you and your clothing.

2 **Be polite.** If you do happen to encounter a gorilla in a bad mood, don't raise your voice. Keep your arms to your side so he thinks that he's large and in charge.

3 **Get dramatic.** If a gorilla charges at you, show him you know who's boss. Act like a scared little kid (as if you need to act).

4 **Ape escape.** Now, wait until the gorilla loses interest in you, or until help arrives.

5 **Primp the chimp.** If the great ape calms down, offer your services as a groomer. Caress the fur on his arm, while keeping your fingers crossed that the gorilla doesn't see you as a threat.

HURRICANES

Katrina, Andrew, Rita, and Hugo…sounds like your class list. Actually, these are the hurricanes that have hit the United States with a vengeance in recent years, demolishing cities and lives in their wake. If you can't hightail it out of a hurricane hub, here's how to survive the storm surge.

Blown Away

A hurricane forms over warm waters (at least 80°F, or 27°C) near the equator and generally travels from east to west—a hurricane in the Atlantic Ocean often begins as a thunderstorm off the coast of Africa. The combination of heat and moisture, along with the right wind conditions, creates this wild weather. A hurricane begins as a tropical storm but officially becomes a hurricane once its wind speed reaches 74 miles (120 km) per hour, sometimes reaching wind speeds of over 160 miles (257 km) per hour.

Eye's on You

This giant, spiraling storm swirls around an "eye" at the center. The eye is the calmest part. It has light winds and fair weather. When the eye passes over, you may think the worst is over. But don't believe your eyes. You're only halfway to safety. Some of the strongest wind, rain, and storm surges can occur on the backside of the eye.

Know Your ABCs

The first hurricane of the season gets a name that begins with A, and so on down the alphabet. There are six different name lists that alternate each year, one for each part of the world that gets struck by these swirling menaces. Hurricanes are also rated using a scale from 1 to 5 called the Saffir-Simpson scale. A Category 5 hurricane is the most destructive. When a hurricane does significant damage, its name is retired and replaced. Hazel (1954), Betsy (1965), Anita (1977), Gilbert (1988), Bob (1991), and Ike (2008) are some of the retirees.

FAST FACT • Storms like hurricanes happen in several of the world's oceans. In the Western Pacific Ocean, they are called typhoons; in the Indian Ocean and the Bay of Bengal, they are called cyclones.

Hurricanes are on average 300 miles (483 km) wide.

HOW TO SURVIVE A HURRICANE

1 **Be prepared.** When you catch wind of an approaching hurricane, stock up on batteries, a battery-operated radio, bottled water, food, tools, and first-aid supplies.

2 **Board it up.** Place wooden boards over windows. The intense winds of a hurricane can blow glass to smithereens or send debris right into your home.

3 **Flee the beach.** If you are near the ocean, get as far inland as possible. Storm surges cause huge waves and flooding (p. 56) in coastal areas.

4 **Get centered.** If you are unable to flee, move to the center part of a building, preferably where there are no windows. The bathroom is a good option.

ICE

If anyone has ever said, "You're skating on thin ice," they're saying you're one false move from disaster. So if you're literally on top of thin ice and it starts cracking, you could wind up a kid-sicle. Before lacing up those skates, check out these stakes.

Don't Cross Me!

There's an old saying about crossing the ice: "Thick and blue, tried and true. Thin and crispy, way too risky." Clear blue or blue-black ice that is free of snow, air bubbles, and debris, like leaves and twigs, is the strongest. Ice that is white, brittle, mixed with snow, or filled with air bubbles isn't as strong. Some people call it "rotten ice" or "you-better-not-even-think-of-setting-foot-on-this-ice ice."

Testing the Waters

The only sure way to know if ice is safe (or not) is to test it. An adult should perform this test by boring a hole into the ice with a drill or cutting it with an ice pick or an axe. Then measure how thick it is with a tape measure. If the ice is less than 5 inches (12.5 cm) thick, don't risk it. If it's 5 inches (12.5 cm) or more, it's time to bust out the skates.

BEWARE

DON'T WALK ON ICE

THIN ICE

BE AWARE • If your friend falls through the ice, don't reach in with your hands or he might pull you in, too. Instead, try to talk him through the steps of getting out. If your friend is really struggling, get a hold of a rope, a hockey stick, or a tree branch and hand him a line. Be sure to stay as far away from the edge as possible and tug your friend to safety.

In cold water, conserving body heat is essential for survival and increasing your chances of being rescued.

DANGER
Thin Ice

HOW TO SURVIVE A FALL THROUGH THIN ICE

1. **Just breathe.** Plunging into freezing water is going to deliver a serious shock to your system. Get your head above water, take some deep breaths, and stay calm.

2. **Backtrack.** Figure out which direction you came from—you must have come from solid ice. Find your footprints and face that way.

3. **Elbow your way out.** Once you've got a grip on some solid ice, get your elbows up on the surface and hoist yourself partly out of the water. Let some of the water weight drain off you before climbing all the way out. If you keep slipping, dig your house keys, or anything else you might have on hand, into the ice for traction.

4. **Roll from the hole.** Do not stand up! Roll away from the hole to spread your weight evenly, and hopefully, keep you from going back into the water.

ICEBERGS

Though iceberg in a salad isn't terribly tasty, it's nothing to fear. Icebergs in the water, however, are big hunks of frozen fright! It was an iceberg that took down the "unsinkable" *Titanic* in 1912 and led to the establishment of the International Ice Patrol. Here's how to stay chill when facing Big 'Berg.

Deep Freeze

An iceberg is a giant chunk of freshwater ice that breaks off from glaciers and ice shelves and sets sail in the ocean. An iceberg comes in all shapes and sizes, ranging from ice cubes, the size of the ones floating in your drink, to ice islands, the size of the country of Luxembourg. The North Atlantic and the cold waters around Antarctica are the happy home to most icebergs.

Chill Out

If you find yourself stranded on an iceberg, the first thing to do is to make a shelter. You can build a trench (a long hole covered by blocks of ice). You can also make yourself at home in a snow cave.

Slushy or Sushi?

The good news about icebergs is that they have plenty of freshwater at the surface. But, of course, it's frozen water. Scrape off as much as you can and put it in a container. Let the sun do the rest. As for curing the munchies, how does sushi sound? Make a fishing rod and eat the catch of the day…raw.

FAST FACT • There's a lot of truth to the expression, "That's just the *tip of the iceberg*." Around 90 percent of the iceberg mass lurks below the surface.

An iceberg in Antarctica. A chunk of ice has to be larger than 16 feet (5 m) across to be an "iceberg."

HOW TO BUILD A SNOW CAVE

1 **Find the right spot.** Look for a spot on the side of a slope with lots of snow. You want snow that is soft enough to dig, but hard enough so your cave won't collapse.

2 **Dig in.** It helps if you have a shovel. Dig an entrance tunnel about 3 feet (0.9 m) straight into the snow bank. Make it big enough to crawl through.

3 **Carve it out.** Carve out the main chamber. Make it big enough so that you can lie down and sit up comfortably.

POOT

4 **Poke a hole.** Poke a hole in the roof of your new snow cave all the way through to the outside. Breathe in that fresh air.

JELLYFISH

It's brainless, boneless, and has no heart. And though it might seem hard to believe that this semi-clear, floating puddle of jelly could cause you any harm, it can sting you like a hive of angry bees. Here are some tips to help you deal with this heartless creature.

Multi-Armed and Dangerous

Most jellyfish have tentacles. The number of tentacles varies, ranging from as few as eight to hundreds. These tentacles are equipped with *nematocysts*, tiny structures in the cells that deliver a sting by firing tiny "darts" of venom. There can be thousands of nematocysts lining the tentacles of a jellyfish. Ouch!

Tentacle Power

A jellyfish uses its tentacles to grab its prey. Once the venom has killed the prey, the tentacles help move the food to the jellyfish's hungry mouth. The tentacles also help a jellyfish defend itself. Even if the sting doesn't kill a predator, it can paralyze it long enough for the jellyfish to escape.

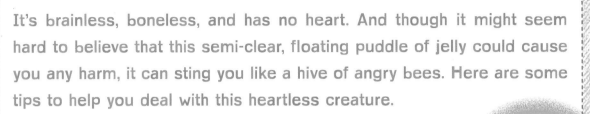

Jellyfish have little control over their horizontal movement, and tend to drift in the ocean currents. A jellyfish can move up and down, however, by contracting its bell (the head).

Too Many to Count

Jellyfish are found in all oceans and seas. There are so many species it's impossible to know exactly how many different kinds there are. Plus, new species are being discovered yearly. Some species are smaller than your thumbnail. The world's largest known jellyfish can reach a diameter of 8 feet (2.5 m). Its tentacles can grow to be half the length of a football field!

FAST FACT • The box jellyfish, or sea wasp, (found off the northern Australian coast) kills more people than any other marine creature each year. Between 1954 and 1996 there were 5,567 recorded deaths related to this jellyfish. A sting from a box jellyfish can kill a person in less than 60 seconds.

A school of jellyfish is called a "smack."

HOW TO TREAT A JELLYFISH STING

1. **Don't be fresh.** You want to rinse the sting right away, but only use seawater. Salt lessens the sting. Freshwater will actually make the sting feel worse.

2. **Dress the wound.** Dress your wound like a salad and douse it with vinegar. The acid in vinegar helps to deactivate those nasty nematocysts. You can also use mustard in a pinch—it's chock-full of vinegar.

3. **Lift off!** If you still have any stingers on you, lift them off with a stick or gloved hand. Don't scrape them off or you'll cause more stinging.

4. **Pass on the pee.** You may have heard that peeing on a sting will ease the pain. Studies have shown this doesn't really work. Phew!

JUNGLES

So, Tarzan or Jane, you've found yourself lost in the jungle, or actually in a tropical rain forest. Jungles are areas with the most overgrown mess of vines in and around a rain forest. They are often found on the edges of the forest or near water sources. The reason they're so thick with plant growth is that they let in more light than other parts of the rain forest, making them lush, plush, and full of creepy, crawly underbrush.

Welcome to the Jungle

The jungle is home to many frightening creatures, including jaguars, anacondas, and vipers. Believe it or not, the larger animals are probably more scared of you than you are of them. It's the little guys—scorpions, ants, flies, and mosquitoes—that you need to worry about. Also, avoid any brightly colored creatures, like the poison dart frog. Bright colors are nature's way of saying, "WARNING! POISON!"

Water Works

One good thing about being lost in a rain forest is that there's rain! Collect fresh rainwater in any kind of vessel. If you don't feel like waiting around for the rain to fill up your cup, you can drink water straight from a vine. Water vines are thick, round vines from the grape family that are usually full of water. Make a notch as high as you can reach, then cut off the bottom at a low point. Lift the vine to your mouth and drink up!

What's Cookin'?

What should you eat with all of that water? Bugs! Look for grubs, worms, and termites beneath rotting logs and plants. Pinch off the heads, imagine you're eating popcorn, and pop them into your mouth. Who needs butter? Avoid insects that are brightly colored, stinky, or hairy.

When the leaf canopy at the top of a rain forest develops gaps, the rampant undergrowth that springs up causes a jungle.

HOW TO FIND CIVILIZATION

1. **Find me a river.** Keep an eye out for animal trails. These often lead to water sources.

2. **Leave bread crumbs.** Just like Hansel and Gretel, mark your own trail as you walk through the jungle. Break or turn over fresh vegetation. The bright undersides of leaves will be noticeable if you need to backtrack.

3. **Take it easy.** If the weather's bad or you need to rest, set up shelter. Look for a clearing and make a lean-to: place large sticks at an angle against a fallen tree or rock, then use some large leaves to fill the holes and line the ground. Now, you've got a first-class suite.

DO NOT DISTURB

4. **Head downstream.** Once you reach a river, walk downstream (the direction in which the water is flowing). People usually live near water, so look for clues of inhabitation—cleared paths, drinking containers, and any man-made materials. Then yell, "Help!"

KILLER WHALES

Killer whales are lean, mean hunting machines, making them among the most fearsome predators in the ocean. Up to 32 feet (9.7 m) long (that's about the length of 2 SUVs) and weighing up to 6 tons (5,443 kg), killer whales hunt in packs, "talk" to each other over long distances, swim at speeds up to 35 mph (50 kph), and have been known to toss around their prey before eating it. Do you want to be the one to tell them not to play with their food?

Name Game

Killer whales are actually more closely related to dolphins than to whales. They are the largest members of the dolphin family. Their real name is orca. But that's not to say orcas don't deserve the nickname "killer." Orcas have powerful jaws and sharp teeth as long as 4 inches (10 cm). They eat up to 500 pounds (227 kg) of food daily and snack on fish, penguins, seals, and even other whales. These ferocious hunters have been known to catch a seal, bat it around, and do belly flops on it before sinking their teeth in.

Orcas navigate using echolocation—that is, bouncing sounds off objects to figure out where those objects are.

In Black and White

The black and white coloration of the killer whale is the perfect camouflage for these gigantic hunters. When seen from above, the black back mixes well with the dark water beneath them. When seen from below, the white belly blends with the sunlit water above them. Unfortunately, if you're a seal, you might not see them coming at all.

Pod Power

Orcas travel in family groups called pods. A typical pod is 5 to 30 whales, though larger pods have been seen. Each pod hunts together and has distinct ways of "talking" to each other while they plan an attack. Small pods sometimes unite to form a larger clan.

MAP OF ORCA'S RANGE

NORTH AMERICA

EUROPE

ASIA

AFRICA

SOUTH AMERICA

AUSTRALIA

ANTARCTICA

BE AWARE
Wild orcas are not considered a threat to humans. However, whales in captivity have been known to injure their trainers. Keep your distance!

A killer whale breaches the surface, thrusting most of its body out of the water and splashing down again.

KOMODO DRAGONS

Giant fire-breathing dragons may be the stuff of myths and magical children's songs, but dragons aren't just imaginary creatures—they're real! On Indonesia's islands (yes, by the sea), you'll find the Komodo dragon, the world's largest reptile, which can grow up to 10 feet (3m) long and weigh 300 pounds (136 kg)! If you're not scared yet, keep reading.

Captain Crunch

A carnivore with a dragon-sized appetite, the Komodo dragon hunts and kills large prey, like pigs and deer. They even have been known to take down water buffalo…and people. The good news is that a Komodo doesn't need to feed often. A large one can survive on as little as twelve filling meals a year—partly because it gulps down almost every bit of its prey, including fur, feathers, hooves, and antlers.

Dragon Breath

A Komodo dragon has powerful legs and super-sharp claws. It also has sixty sharp, serrated teeth, perfect for tearing flesh— imagine a mouthful of steak knives. A Komodo dragon's bite is also filled with venom that is pumped into its mouth through poison glands. If the teeth don't kill you first, the deadly drool will.

Takes a Licking

The Komodo finds most of its food using its sense of smell. But it's not sniffing with its nose. A Komodo dragon "smells" the air using its long, yellow, forked tongue. It walks along, swinging its head from side to side, with its tongue hanging out. The tongue picks up chemicals from the air, then a special organ inside the mouth tells the dragon which way the food is. It can detect dinner from as far away as 5 miles (8 km).

Light-footed Lizards

You might think they move slowly, but these dreaded dragons can move quickly. They can run about 13 miles (21 km) per hour. If one is after you, don't jump in the water! Komodo dragons are good swimmers. They swish their long tails back and forth to propel themselves through the water—a lot faster than your kicking legs will take you! So if you're in Komodo country, keep your eyes peeled, and keep moving.

FAST FACT • Komodo dragons are cannibals—they *will* eat their own kind. Adult dragons think young hatchlings make a tasty treat. As soon as a dragon hatches and crawls out of its nest, it faces danger. To keep safe, hatchlings scramble up trees, a smart move since the adults are too heavy to climb trees. Another strategy for a young Komodo is to roll itself up in poop, so the adults can't smell it.

A Komodo dragon lazily walks along a forest path on Komodo Island, Indonesia.

LIGHTNING

Despite popular belief, lightning *can* strike twice. So unless you want your teeth to shatter or the soles of your shoes to melt, it's best to avoid getting struck even once. When thunder starts crackin', don't dally outdoors. It's not worth the risk of having something shocking happen to you!

It's Electric

Lightning is a bright flash of electricity produced by a thunderstorm. Within thunderclouds, tiny bits of ice swirl around and bang into each other. These collisions create an electrical charge. It's like the charge that can build up when you walk on a carpet in socks, but *a lot* stronger.

Kapow!

During a storm, thunderclouds fill up with these electrical charges. Positive charges form at the top; negative charges form at the bottom. Because opposites attract, a positive charge builds up on the ground below the cloud. This positive charge is especially powerful around anything sticking up. Think mountains, trees, and golfers swinging a club. The charged-up cloud "wants" to complete the electrical circuit, so a bolt reaches down from the clouds. *Kapow*—lightning strikes! The super heat of the bolt causes the air around it to explode with a boom—you guessed it, thunder.

Shockingly Serious

Every year, lightning kills an estimated 10,000 people worldwide. That's more deaths than result from tornados and hurricanes. Around 100,000 people are struck by lightning every year and live to tell the tale. But they can wind up with some serious health problems, including internal burns and even brain damage.

Gimme Shelter

If you see lightning, run for cover! Make that double time if you feel a tingling sensation or your hair standing on end. If you're not close to shelter, stay away from tall trees, poles, open areas, water, and anything metal. Get on all fours and lay low until the storm is over. (And keep your mouth closed if you've got braces!)

How far away is a storm? Count the number of seconds between when you see lightning and hear thunder, then divide by five. This will give you the distance in miles. For kilometers, divide the number of seconds by three. (If you count ten seconds between lightning and thunder, the lightning is 2 miles, or 3.2 km, away!)

A bolt of lightning can travel at speeds of 140,000 miles (220,000 km) per hour and reach temperatures approaching 54,000°F (30,000°C).

LIONS

Rule of thumb: When you encounter something that weighs 500 pounds (227 kg) called the "king of the jungle," don't be the joker who bothers him. Despite the "jungle" nickname, most lions live in the desert, or where there's grassland, scrub, and open woodlands. But no need to be the joker who mocks the king's moniker, either!

Have Some Pride

Lions are the coolest cats around. They are the only social members of the cat family and often live in groups called "prides." Each pride has about fifteen lions, mostly related females and their young. A single male or a small group of males may join a pride for a while. That is, until another big boy takes over. Lions within a pride interact with each other by head rubbing, licking, and purring.

The Mane Event

Male lions are very protective and patrol a very large area around its pride. They roar loudly—a lion's roar can be heard from

LION RANGE MAP

AFRICA

5 miles (8 km) away—and chase off animals that threaten their turf. Males also mark their territory with a healthy dose of urine. Nothing says "back off" like lion pee.

You Go, Girl!

Male lions may be powerful, but when it comes to hunting, they're better off staying at home and washing their manes. Lionesses do most of the hunting at night, working in teams to hunt prey, including zebras and antelopes.

FAST FACT • Lions are not only found in Africa. A small population of lions with a little over 400 members (and growing) lives in Gir National Park in the Gujarat region of India.

Rowr!!!
An African lion
...to warn

HOW TO SURVIVE A LION ENCOUNTER

1 **Motor it.** Lions will rarely attack humans, but if one does, you're in big trouble. If you see a lion, you're most likely on a safari. In this case, walk backward slowly and get inside the jeep. Roll those windows up! Then yell, "Drive! Drive!" and hope someone listens.

2 **Face forward.** The worst thing to do is act like prey, so don't turn your back on the lion and run away. Lions can run up to 50 miles (80 km) per hour over short distances. That's as fast as a speeding car on the highway.

3 **Act tough.** If you come face-to-face with a lion, stand up tall, flap your arms, and scream. Hopefully, this will confuse the lion, since its usual prey of zebras, wildebeests, and buffalo don't typically act this way.

MOBS

You scored tickets to the biggest sporting event of the year. The crowd is pumped, and energy and emotions are running high. All of a sudden, a spark turns that previously cool crowd red-hot, and then the unquiet riot begins...

Mob Mentality

The intense excitement of a political protest, a big sporting event, or even a mega-star signing autographs can turn a lively crowd into an unruly mob scene. Instead of looking out for others, people in a mob run right over each other. People have even been hurt while shopping. "Doorbuster" sales often find shoppers camped outside the stores until the doors open early in the morning. The rush of people charging into the stores has resulted in injuries and even deaths.

Just For Kicks?

Believe it or not, mobs at soccer games have helped start wars—more than once. El Salvador and Honduras went to war with each other for four days after a series of heated riots at soccer matches in 1969. This brief war is known as the Football War. In 1990, there was a match between a Croatian club and a Serbian club that turned into a riot—the hostilities played a part in beginning the Croatian War of Independence.

IN A FLASH

A flash mob is a large group of people who show up at the same place at the same time. The event is planned beforehand, usually on the Internet. The people participating in the flash mob arrive on the scene, then do something totally wacky, like break into a song or dance routine. When finished, they disperse as quickly as they gathered.

FAST FACT

Major political and social changes have often started with riots, when mobs have erupted to fight authority or demand change.

HOW TO SURVIVE A MOB

1 **Make an exit strategy.**
If you are in a crowded place, know where the exits are and the fastest way to get to them. Be sensitive to the mood of the crowd. If you see angry behavior or fights breaking out, get to the edges and think about making an early exit.

2 **Stay neutral.** Don't get involved or take sides, even if someone is cursing your favorite team. You don't want the angry mob to direct its anger at *you*.

3 **Get out.** If it's too late and you're caught in a mob, go with the flow, while trying to work your way out of the crowd. Don't go against the direction of the mob and don't try to run out of it—you'll just be more likely to get knocked down.

4 **Roll up.** If you do fall down, roll up into a ball. Put your arms around your head and pull your knees up to your chest to protect yourself from being trampled.

MOSQUITOES

Pop Quiz: What's the world's deadliest animal? A. Lions B. Vipers C. Polar Bears D. Mosquitoes. If you answered D, you get an A! By transmitting diseases through bites, the miniscule mosquito is responsible for killing millions (yes, millions) of people each year. And you thought all that buzzing and itching was just annoying!

Menacing Malaria

When it comes to diseases, malaria is a monster. Malaria has killed more people than all of the other diseases on Earth combined. During the last 100 years, major efforts to reduce mosquito populations have eliminated malaria from North America, Australia, and Europe. But it's still a major problem in sub-Saharan Africa, South America, and South Asia. Every year, between 200 and 500 million people get malaria and between 2 and 3 million people die from the disease.

So Much Torment…So Little Time

A mosquito can grow from egg to an adult in as little as 5 days. Once mature, female mosquitoes rarely live beyond 2 weeks. For males, 1 week is a long, healthy life. They make up for this short lifespan by breeding like crazy. On average, a female mosquito can lay anywhere from 1,000 to 3,000 eggs. Only the female mosquito bites. She needs a "blood meal" to feed her legions of offspring.

BE AWARE • The best way to swat a mosquito is to use two hands. Mosquitoes may be able to avoid one hand, but when the second one shows up, their tiny brains get confused. They may be deadly, but they're still pretty dumb.

What Are They Good For?

Absolutely nothing? Not quite. Mosquitoes are a good source of food for other animals. Fish, frogs, bats, lizards, dragonflies, and birds love to feast on these bloodsuckers. Also, mosquitoes of both sexes feed on the nectar of plants. This makes them good pollinators. But do we really need them? Maybe not. No animal feeds *exclusively* on mosquitoes and there is no plant that *depends* on mosquitoes for pollination.

HOW TO AVOID MOSQUITOES

1 **Stay inside.** Mosquitoes are most active at dawn and dusk. So hang inside during these times of the day. It's too early to be up at dawn anyway!

2 **Cover up.** If you are outside, mosquitoes will be less likely to bite you if you're wearing lightly colored, loose-fitting clothing that has long sleeves and pant legs.

3 **Slather it on.** As its name implies, a mosquito repellant *repels* those pesky blood feeders. Repellants come in many different forms, including sprays, lotions, and gels. Always have an adult help you apply repellant.

4 **Get a net.** A mosquito net is one of the easiest—and inexpensive—ways to keep mosquitoes at bay. Sleeping under a mosquito net lowers one's risk of catching malaria by 50 percent.

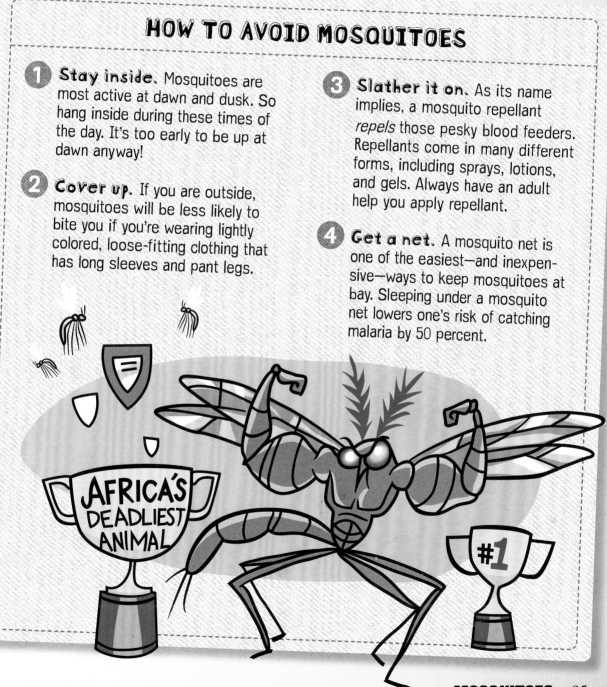

AFRICA'S DEADLIEST ANIMAL

#1

MOUNTAIN LIONS

Q: If both mountains and lions are dangerous, how should you greet a mountain lion? A: Very carefully! **Cougars, pumas, panthers, catamounts, and mountain screamers are all mountain lions, and these big cats are often hungry. Fortunately, they don't usually feast on people. So to avoid being the exception, read carefully.**

Big Kitties

They might be called *lions*, but mountain lions look more like house cats than the majestic lions of Africa and Asia. But don't put out a saucer of milk just yet. Mountain lions can take down animals up to seven times their size, including moose and elk, though deer are their favorite snack. Comparatively, that makes you little more than a potentially tasty morsel!

Leaps and Bounds

Cougars are crazy jumpers. An adult can soar as high as 18 feet (5.5 m) in the air and leap about 40 feet (12 m) across the ground. That's enough jumping power to clear a school bus in a single bound—the long way! They're fast, too. In an all-out sprint, a mountain lion can reach speeds up to 45 miles (72 km) per hour.

The Long Ranger

Mountain lions thrive in a wide variety of habitats. Cougar country extends all across North and South America (that's why they have so many names!). They live in western Canada's snowy peaks, in Mexico's deserts, and in South America's rain forests. They don't live in the eastern United States…any longer. The eastern cougar was driven away by humans about one hundred years ago. But there are rumors and unconfirmed sightings that mountain lions are making a stealthy return to their eastern homes. At least sixty of these fierce kitties still exist in Florida, where they are known as Florida panthers.

Mountain lions have stronger back legs than front legs, giving them their jumping power.

Not only good jumpers, mountain lions are also adept at climbing trees.

HOW TO SURVIVE A MOUNTAIN LION ENCOUNTER

1 **Stand tall.** Mountain lions will attack just about anything on four legs, but a creature with two legs may give them pause. Don't sit, crouch, lie down, crawl, or drop to your knees and beg for mercy.

2 **Puff yourself up.** Open your jacket wide to appear bigger than you are. Wave your arms around and shout. Convince this cat that you are not to be messed with.

3 **Look away.** You want to look fearsome, but don't try to stare down a mountain lion. It will just think you're challenging it.

4 **Back it up.** Resist the urge to run. All cats love a good chase. Back away slowly, and don't trip!

5 **If all else fails...fight!** With sticks, with stones, with fists—go for the feline's eyes and mouth. Try to stay upright (this cat wants your neck!) and don't give up. It won't take pity on you.

ROAR!

MOUNTAINS

Ah, wilderness! As you climb to the top of the mountain, you're enchanted by treetops, chomping on trail mix, and breathing the clear mountain air, when the terrain gets tricky without warning. Suddenly you're knee-deep in trail trouble. But with a cool head and the proper gear, you'll be comin' round the mountain in no time.

DON'T

DO

Layer It On

The key to a successful mountain adventure is to stay warm and dry. Dress in three layers. The inner layer should be a "breathable" material that absorbs moisture from your skin. The middle layer should trap and create warm air. The outer layer should let moisture out, but not in. This layer needs to protect you from the elements.

Get in Gear

Your gear needs to be light enough to carry comfortably, but still include what you need to survive. Your minimum mountain checklist: water—approximately ½ gallon (2 L) per day (more if it's hot); nutritious food, such as trail mix, protein bars, and jerky; a smart phone with GPS capability; a Swiss Army knife; a space blanket with a foil-like coating, colored orange on one side; a flashlight; a lighter; a whistle; a mirror; bug spray; and sunscreen.

FAST FACT • If you have a watch, you can tell direction without a compass.

South

1 Hold watch so hour hand points at the sun.

2 Imagine a line halfway between the hour hand and 12—it points south.

HOW TO SURVIVE BEING LOST IN THE MOUNTAINS

1 Fight the fear. Being lost can be scary, but don't panic. Stay calm, and look for a place to shelter. Don't try to push through to the top (it's coldest up there) or make it down to the bottom (cold air falls, and the valleys can be pretty chilly). You told someone where you were going, so rescuers will be looking for you.

2 Take cover. You'll need to have some kind of shelter. Don't try to build a log cabin—that will tire you out and make you sweat too much. Instead, use leaves and branches to make a lean-to (p. 73), and cover it with your space blanket. If you're in the snow, try building a trench or cave (p. 69).

3 Sun up, sign up. Use your mirror to reflect the sun—the flashes can be seen from miles away. If you see a rescue plane or helicopter overhead, aim your signal directly at it: Hold one hand out in front of you and form a "V" between your thumb and index finger. Move your hand until the plane is in the "V." With your other hand, orient the mirror so that the reflected sunlight is shining through the "V" at the object.

A hiker takes in the view from a rocky ledge in Minnesota's Arrowhead region in the United States.

MUDSLIDES

Think sliding into home plate gets you good and dirty? Imagine being chased by a raging avalanche of sludge—good luck on laundry day after that one! Of course, mudslides cause loads and loads of trouble. When a big slide starts, it can take down everything in its path, including trees, homes, and people.

Cars and homes damaged from El Niño storms, Southern California, United States..

When It Rains, It Pours—Mud

Heavy rains from hurricanes (p. 64) and thunderstorms, as well as melting snow, often cause mudslides. When rain soaks the earth on a hillside, it can turn solid ground into a river of mud. Earthquakes (p. 46) and volcanos (p. 130) have also been known to be triggers.

BE AWARE • If you live in an area prone to mudslides, sleep upstairs on rainy nights, even if your bedroom is on the ground floor. Many mudslide-related deaths have occurred while people were asleep, including over 100 deaths in California.

More than Mud

Getting caught in a mudslide isn't like taking a relaxing mud bath. When a mudslide gets moving, rocks, trees, cars, and all sorts of dangerous objects get caught in the mix, forming a "debris flow" or "debris avalanche." Giant boulders get tossed around like pebbles. Entire homes are swept away in a flash.

A Devastating Slide

In 1999, Venezuela saw one of the deadliest mudslides in history. Known as the Vargas tragedy, this series of mudslides was triggered by torrential rain when the area received the amount of two years' worth of rain in two days. The mudslides claimed between 10,000 and 30,000 lives. Entire neighborhoods were completely destroyed, leaving tens of thousand of people homeless.

HOW TO ESCAPE A MUDSLIDE

1. **Head uphill.** Mudslides start to flow with little or no warning. If there is any danger of a mudslide, get to higher ground as soon as you know something is wrong.

2. **Run perpendicularly.** A mudslide can travel as fast as 35 miles (56 km) per hour, so don't try to outrun it. If you are on the side of a hill when a mudslide starts, run perpendicularly to the flow. Surfing is not recommended.

3. **Get inside and up high.** If you are unable to get above or to the side of the mudslide, get inside a building that has a solid foundation. Once inside, move to the highest floor. Mud and debris may still enter the ground floor.

PIRANHAS

The water feels great as you dog paddle in a peaceful river in South America. And those ripples in the distance don't bother you at all, until hundreds of sharp teeth are snapping at your toes. A school of hungry piranhas is after you! Here's how to avoid becoming their after-school snack.

Terrifying Teeth

A piranha has razor-sharp, triangular teeth set in very powerful jaws. The top and bottom teeth interlock. These remarkable dental tools help them tear and rip flesh from a fish or small animal in mere seconds. A piranha's teeth are so sharp, they can even cut through a steel fishhook. People of the Amazon region sometimes fashion the piranhas' pearlies into tools.

Blood Bath

Some species, such as the red-bellied piranha, like to dine family style. They will lurk in groups of twenty to thirty fish, hiding in areas with dense vegetation. They then attack their prey in a ferocious fit of thrashing and biting. As soon as there's blood in the water, piranhas enter a feeding frenzy worse than tourists at an all-you-can-eat buffet.

Don't Mess With Daddy

A male piranha digs out a nest for the female's eggs, then guards them fiercely. Even after the little terrors are born, both parents protect their brood. Red-bellied piranhas spawn in the rainy season of April and May. Even though piranhas are deadlier during the dry season, that probably isn't a great time to go poking around in the Amazon River, either.

PIRANHA ANATOMY

SKIN: Secretes a mucus that's for protection, as well as helping it move quickly through the water.

CAUDAL FIN: Helps propel the piranha.

TEETH: Are used for weapons by South American natives.

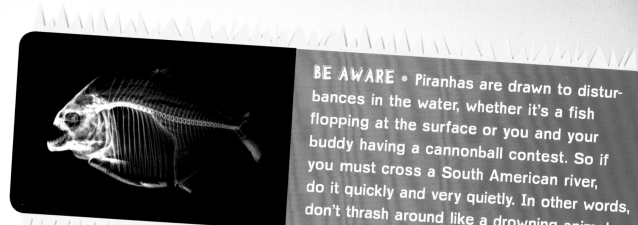

HOW TO CROSS PIRANHA-INFESTED WATERS

1 **Ditch the docks.** Stay away from docks where people catch, cut, and clean fish. These bloody spots are like fast-food restaurants for piranhas.

2 **Flee the frenzy.** If you see the water bubbling or churning, don't go in! Piranhas generally eat prey smaller than you are. But don't get in their way—you may get a nasty bite. Let the feisty little feeders eat in peace.

3 **Be nocturnal.** Piranhas are most active at dawn, so avoid rivers at daybreak. They are also active at dusk, or sundown. They are least active at night. So if you must cross piranha-infested waters, the nighttime is the right time.

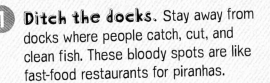

POISON PLANTS

Wicked thorns, sharp blades, and fast-acting poisons—yes, even plants have self-defense systems! And among plants' protective weaponry are some poisonous chemicals that pose major dangers—merely touching some of these can leave you itchy, oozy, and miserable, while just a taste of others can be deadly. So before you go rolling in the greenery or start munching on some nice-looking berries, get the scoop on the vicious vegetation.

Rash Masters

Three of the most infamous poison plants are poison ivy, poison oak, and poison sumac. These three have one very nasty thing in common: urushiol, an oily sap found in all parts of the plants. When urushiol comes in contact with skin, it can cause a terribly itchy rash. One helpful hint for avoiding poisonous plants is, "Leaves of three, let it be." Unfortunately, this handy rhyme applies only to poison ivy and poison oak. For poison sumac, you're on your own; it has seven to thirteen leaves. It does have clusters of drooping green berries, so if you see any plants matching this description, stay away.

Execution by Plant

With its lacy leaves and delicate white flowers, hemlock might not look scary. But this common plant (also known as "poison parsley" and "devil's porridge") is lethal. Found on every continent except South America and Antarctica, hemlock was used by the ancient Greeks to execute convicted criminals—the most famous being Socrates, who was given a deathly dose of hemlock tea, leading to paralysis and death. The leaves and roots, when crushed, smell awful— so if it stinks, don't drink!

BE AWARE • If your pets run around in wooded areas where they could brush up against poison plants, wash your hands after petting them. They can carry urushiol on their fur, then that oily fur can rub off on *you.*

POISON PLANTS

POISON IVY
Captain John Smith first wrote about poison ivy in the early 1600s.

POISON OAK
This plant only lives below an elevation of 5,000 feet (1,500 m).

POISON SUMAC
This poison plant grows in standing water, like peats bogs and swamps.

HOW TO TREAT POISON IVY, OAK, AND SUMAC

1 **Wash it off.** If you even *think* you have been exposed to a poisonous plant, get home and strip down. Put all your clothes in the wash, then take a cold shower. Avoid hot water because it opens up your pores and allows the urushiol to seep in deeper.

2 **Don't scratch.** Scratching the rash will not spread it. Only having urushiol on your hands can spread the rash. However, you can give yourself a nasty infection if you scratch too much.

3 **Cool it.** Once the blisters rear their ugly little heads, there isn't much you can do. Cooling and soothing the rash with cold showers, cool compresses, or lukewarm oatmeal baths can reduce the pain and itching somewhat. Follow with a drying lotion, such as calamine.

QUICKSAND

You don't have to wonder what quicksand will do to you. "Quicksand" tells it like it is: You step on what looks like solid sand, then start sinking quickly! This watery sand, clay, and salt mixture feels kind of like thick mud soup. But if you know its secret, you won't wind up stuck in the muck.

Bottomless Pit?

Quicksand is dangerous stuff, but it isn't as bad as you might think. For one thing, quicksand is rarely more than three feet (1 m) deep. It is easy to stumble into quicksand, but it is difficult to sink below your waist. Quicksand's real danger is that it traps people. Once you're trapped, it's easy to succumb to other hazards, like a rising tide or the scorching sun.

Think Like a Boat and Float

Even if you fall into an unusually deep pit of quicksand, it won't swallow you whole. The truth is that people can actually float in quicksand. In fact, you float better in quicksand than you do in regular water because humans are less dense than quicksand. So if you find yourself sinking, lean back. Spread your arms and legs to distribute your weight and make it easier to float.

DRY QUICKSAND, FAKE? NOT SO FAST!

Don't Fight It

The scary thing about quicksand is that the more you struggle, the faster you sink. When you lift your foot in quicksand, it creates a vacuum. This vacuum pulls back down on your foot with surprising force. So don't panic. The trick is to wriggle slowly. If you keep your movements wriggly, you can fill the vacuum with water. This will make it possible for you to move, although very slowly. Patience also helps.

"Dry quicksand," the kind you see in movies, has never been found, but scientists have created it in a laboratory. And they say there's no reason why it couldn't form naturally. Dry quicksand is created by flowing air through very fine sand, then letting it settle. When you drop an object into dry quicksand it falls so fast that it actually makes a splash!

RIP CURRENTS

One minute you're frolicking in the sea, the next you're being sucked away from shore as if a sea monster is slurping you into a straw. You've just met a rip current. Rip currents are narrow channels of water flowing rapidly out to sea. Usually, sand slows them down, but if there's a dip in the sandbar, it's a fast track off shore.

AVOID THE RIP CURRENT

Escape the Grip of the Rip

The reason rip currents are so deadly is that many people don't understand how they work. A rip current moves pretty fast—faster than you can swim. When people try to swim against a rip current, it's like swimming on a treadmill. No matter how hard you swim, you won't make it any closer to shore. In the end, people wind up too exhausted to swim anymore, and they drown.

Current Events

Rip currents, often mistakenly called riptides, can occur in any kind of weather, and on any beach with breaking waves. Weather conditions that are rip-current friendly include very windy days and approaching storms. All beaches—including those of large lakes, such as North America's Great Lakes—have experienced rip currents.

Ripped from the Headlines

Rip currents can form at any time, but there are some warning signs that one might be lurking: a streak of muddy water heading out to sea, a rippled stripe of water, or crisscrossed waves can all indicate a possible rip current. Swim where lifeguards are on duty; they will have up-to-date info on the rips.

HOW TO SURVIVE A RIP CURRENT

1. **Swim sideways.** Don't try to fight the current. You will lose. Instead, swim parallel to the shore until you are out of the current.

2. **Go with the flow.** If you cannot swim out of the current, simply float on your back. Try to save your energy. After 50 to 100 yards (46 to 91 m), the rip current should stop pulling you out to sea.

3. **On the beach.** Even if you are being taken out to sea, stay calm. If there are people on shore, wave your hands and yell. Rip currents occur close enough to shore for someone on the beach to see or hear you, and get help.

4. **Be an angler.** Once you are out of the rip current, swim back to shore at an angle *away* from the rip current. You certainly don't want to go through *that* again.

BE AWARE • The good news is that rip currents aren't very big. A typical rip current is less than 100 feet (30.5 m) wide and rarely extends more than 100 yards (91 m) from shore.

RUNAWAY HORSES

She might have seemed laid-back when you climbed into the saddle, but something has really spooked your steed. Suddenly, she's galloping like a champion in the final stretch of a high-stakes race. Here's how to find your inner horse whisperer and get this filly under control.

Off and Running

Each horse has its own list of personal goblins and many can be "spooked" easily. Some things that commonly scare horses are loud or sudden noises, other animals, windy weather, snakes, and even puddles of water. When scared, or even irritated, horses usually react in the same way— they bolt. If a horse bolts while you're on it, you're not exactly going to get a joyride.

Horses often bolt when they are frightened, but sometimes simply because they are tempted by the prospect of running free.

Serious Horsepower

A full-grown horse is a powerful animal, weighing up to 2,200 pounds (998 kg) and capable of galloping at a speed of 30 miles (48 km) per hour. If it's galloping toward you, get out of its way, or it'll be like a small car rolled over you.

Whoa, Nellie!

If you sense a horse getting spooked or irritated, remain in control. Staying calm will help your horse. Be a de-stress-or for your equine pal. Talk in a calm, reassuring voice. Rub its neck gently with one hand. The last thing you want to do is yell, scream, or kick. Doing this will only end with you careening off into the distance at breakneck speed.

HOW TO STOP A RUNAWAY HORSE

1 **Hold on.** Grip the saddle tightly with your hands and thighs. Hold onto the reins with one hand and the saddle horn with the other (or use both hands to grip the horn if you've lost the reins). Most injuries happen when a rider is thrown, falls, or jumps off—so hold on for dear life.

2 **Sit back.** Resist the urge to lean forward, which may be tough if you're streaking through the woods! Sit back and deep in the seat, grip the horse with your thighs, and firmly say "Whoa." This tells the horse you want to stop.

3 **Tug.** Tug and release the reins with medium pressure, over and over. You're telling the horse you want to slow down. Never jerk the reins because this could cause you to fall off or the horse to fall… or both.

4 **Get off.** When the horse finally stops, dismount right away before that horse can bolt again! Swing one leg over the horse so you've got both your legs on one side. Balance on your hands on the saddle, and kick the other foot out of the stirrup. Push lightly away, and drop to the ground. Move quickly out of kick range.

WHOA!

SANDSTORMS

When the sand starts swirling, you could be in the Sahara, Sudan, Seoul, or even Sydney, but you won't be able to tell by looking. When the winds whip and the particles begin to fly, they can swiftly form clouds so dense, they block out the sun.

Dust in the Wind

Sometimes, dust is the culprit, not sand. Areas where the land is especially dry can suffer from dust storms, when gusts of wind lift vast amounts of dirt particles into the air, forming giant walls of dust. These dust storms have been known to travel and even envelop cities, including Melbourne and Dallas, located hundreds of miles from where the dust originated.

Sands of No Time

In the desert, particularly the Sahara, sandstorms can blow up in an instant. Especially between April and August, fierce, hot desert winds with speeds of 60 miles (96 km) per hour can whip up tons of sand and carry it across the land—even moving entire dunes.

The Scene from Above

Some sandstorms are so big, they can be seen from space. In March 2010, a massive sandstorm that originated in Inner Mongolia sent dust and sand as far as Beijing, Taiwan, and even Japan. Satellite images revealed that it could be clearly seen from space.

Sand swirls near the pyramids at Giza, in Egypt.

A dune in Africa's central Namib desert.

HOW TO SURVIVE A SAND OR DUST STORM

1 Cover up. The winds will force sand up your nose, into your eyes, and even past your tightly closed lips. Use a scarf or bandanna to cover up your mouth and nose—this works even better if you dampen it first. Wear goggles or sunglasses to protect your eyes.

2 Stay together. One of the scariest things about sandstorms is how they can blind you. One second, you're looking at your buddy, the next second, you can't see a thing. If you see sand approaching, link arms with everyone you're with so no one gets lost. If you have a rope, make everyone grab on.

3 Turn away. If you can't find shelter, get down and face away from the wind. If you have a vehicle, whether it's a car or a camel, get behind it until the storm passes.

SCORPIONS

A scorpion wears body armor and glows in the dark (if you shine an ultraviolet light on it). And it can measure over 8 inches (20 cm) long—the width of this page. It uses its claws to capture prey...which should pray for dear life when it gets caught.

The Tale of the Tail

Like spiders, scorpions are arachnids and have eight legs. Most scorpions use their claws to capture prey, like insects and small rodents. But if an animal is difficult to overpower, the scorpion uses its famous stinging tail, which carries the venom. A pair of glands pumps the venom through the stinger when the scorpion strikes, shutting down the victim's nervous system. Only fifty of the couple thousand scorpion species have enough juice to do any real damage to humans.

Super Senses

A scorpion has six to twelve eyes, but it still doesn't see very well. Its eyes are very sensitive to light, so a scorpion prefers to navigate at night, by the light of the moon. The scorpion also uses hairy sensors on its legs and belly to creep around...and find its way into your shoe.

SIGNS OF THE SCORPION

TAIL
Carries the venom glands and the venom-injecting barb.

HAIRY SENSORS
Protrude from the legs and belly to help with navigation.

PINCERS
Grasp and hold prey.

Scorpions are found on all continents except Antarctica.

Tough Stuff

Scorpions are remarkably tough little creatures. Scientists have placed a few in a freezer overnight for a chill session. The next day the scorpions thawed out and walked away as if nothing happened. They can also survive long periods of time without food, even going a whole year on one meal.

Male and female scorpions typically do a circular dance before mating.

HOW TO AVOID A SCORPION STING

1 **Shake it out.** Scorpions like to get cozy under piles of laundry, in shoes, or even in your bed sheets. So if you're hanging where scorpions are known to live, shake these items out before you find yourself with an unwelcome bed buddy.

2 **Leave it alone.** Do not turn over rocks or reach into holes. If you surprise a scorpion, the next surprise will be on *you*.

3 **Flee the scene.** If you see a scorpion, get away from it as fast as you can.

4 **Don't freak.** If a scorpion *does* sting you, stay calm. The poison is designed to get your nervous system in high gear. Most scorpion stings are similar to a bee sting.

5 **Chill out.** First, wash the area with soap and water. To ease any pain, apply an ice pack to the sting site for ten minutes on, then ten minutes off, until the pain lets up.

6 **Get serious.** If you experience a bad reaction, such as numbness, sweating, sickness, or fever, have someone take you to a doctor.

SCUBA DIVING

Swimming with the fishes SCUBA-style makes the ocean your personal aquarium. When you're using a Self-Contained Underwater Breathing Apparatus (which, FYI, is what SCUBA stands for), you essentially have gills on your back, allowing you to breathe freely in the water. But if that O_2 tank "tanks," you might be Scared Cuz Ur (Not) Breathing Air...

Get Schooled

Before you dive, you must take a course from a certified instructor. In many countries, you can take lessons in a pool starting at eight years old. But most places don't allow open-water dives until you are around twelve years old.

Into the Deep

In class, you'll learn how to use all of the equipment and how it affects your body. Because water is denser than air, pressure increases as you move deeper underwater. Your body is mostly water, so when you dive, you'll feel water pressure in your body's air spaces—lungs, sinuses, and ear canals. This pressure is the reason you must learn how to go down and back up slowly. If you don't do this properly, you can get air bubbles in your body or even bloodstream, which may lead to a heart attack or stroke.

Buddy Up

A dive buddy is your all-important partner underwater. You stick close to each other and keep an eye out for any kind of trouble, like equipment problems. Dive buddies communicate using basic underwater signs: going up, going down, OK, out of air, shark!

BE AWARE • The recreational diving limit is 130 feet (40 m). A condition called nitrogen narcosis can affect scuba divers who venture below the depth of 66 feet (20 m). Narcosis leads to giddiness, hallucinations, unconsciousness, and can eventually result in death. Many divers have died trying to set the world record for deep-sea diving.

HOW TO SURVIVE TANK TROUBLE

1 **Use sign language.** Point to your tank as a signal to your dive buddy that you are having a problem.

2 **Share equipment.** Share your buddy's regulator—the mouthpiece you breathe through—by passing it back and forth. Take two breaths, then pass it back.

3 **Ascend slowly.** Keep sharing the regulator as you both slowly swim to the surface, exhaling as you go.

EQUIPMENT

MASK

WEIGHT BELT

AIR TANK

FLIPPERS

DIVE BOOTIES

SHARKS

The shark really gets a bad rap. On average, shark attacks kill about five people a year—more people die from getting hit by a falling coconut—but the hysteria they instill is unrivaled. There's just something about its pointy dorsal fin, razor-sharp teeth, powerful jaw, and cold, dark eyes that make you think twice before taking the plunge.

Ancient Predators

Sharks have been super-efficient predators for a long time. The ancestors of modern sharks swam in the Earth's oceans more than 400 million years ago (take that, dinosaurs!) and they have not changed very much since then. Though most people think of the great white as a typical shark, there are actually lots of different varieties of shark, including the tiny dogfish shark, which may reach 8 inches (20 cm) and the giant whale shark, which measures 60 feet (20 m)! Few are dangerous to humans, but the ones to watch out for are great white sharks, tiger sharks, and bull sharks.

Historical Hysteria

One of the first shark hysterias occurred in the summer of 1916 at the New Jersey shore in the United States. A shark now known as the Matawan "Man-Eater" killed four people in twelve days. Not only did these attacks make national headlines, they also prompted a large-scale shark hunt—and the inspiration for the book (and movie) *Jaws*.

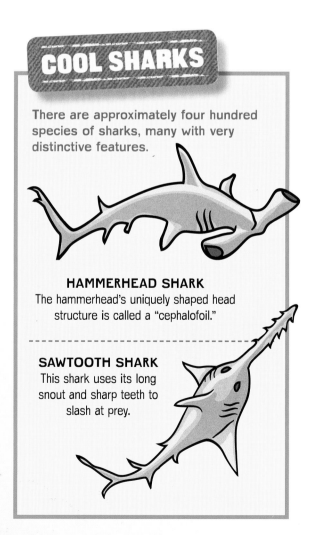

COOL SHARKS

There are approximately four hundred species of sharks, many with very distinctive features.

HAMMERHEAD SHARK
The hammerhead's uniquely shaped head structure is called a "cephalofoil."

SAWTOOTH SHARK
This shark uses its long snout and sharp teeth to slash at prey.

HOW TO SURVIVE A SHARK ATTACK

1. **Attack back.** If you are unlucky enough to be in a shark's sights, you still have a fighting chance. Hit that fearsome fish with everything and anything you've got—fists, feet, camera, harpoon…

2. **Take aim.** You may have heard that you should aim for a shark's nose. This is not necessarily the best spot to shoot for. Go for the shark's gills and eyes. Punch, poke, kick—do whatever it takes to avoid becoming lunch.

3. **Fight, fight, fight.** Keep on hitting that shark where it hurts. Convince the shark that you're not worth the trouble.

4. **Land ho!** Make your way back to the beach as soon as possible. The shark can't follow you onto shore!

At an average length of 16 feet (4.8 m) and weighing about a ton, the great

SHIPWRECKS

The story goes that when the *Titanic* set sail in April 1912, the ship was declared "unsinkable." Well, we all know how that one turned out. So what do you do if your boat doesn't float? Step 1: Stop rearranging the deck chairs. Step 2: Try to make your way to the life rafts. Here's how...

Maritime Mystery

Not all shipwrecks occur out on the open sea. The Great Lakes, which are five large lakes located in North America, have also had their share of disasters. But none are as mysterious (or tragic) as that of the *Edmund Fitzgerald*. On November 9, 1975, the ship set out on Lake Superior from Superior, Wisconsin, with twenty-nine crew members and 26,000 tons (23,587 t) of iron ore destined for Zug Island near Detroit, Michigan. On the afternoon of November 10, the captain radioed to another ship that his ship was having trouble. By that night, the *Edmund Fitzgerald* had split in two and sunk 530 feet (161 m), killing everyone on board. There are lots of theories about why the freighter went down, including bad weather, captain error, structural problems, and even UFOs, but the actual cause is still unknown.

On a Collision Course

You may have heard the saying, "Like two ships passing in the night." But in the case of the SS *Andrea Doria* and the MS *Stockholm*, these were two ships "crashing" in the night. Like the *Titanic*, the *Andrea Doria* was considered an unsinkable, top-of-the-line ocean liner. But on the night of July 25, 1956, the *Stockholm*, which was headed to Sweden, collided with the *Andrea Doria*, which was headed to New York, off the island of Nantucket in the United States. Fortunately, between the two ships, only fifty-one people died in the crash. Captain error is to blame for the accident, though which boat was at fault is still up for debate.

Shipwrecks create habitats for a variety of marine life, and make interesting diving spots.

HOW TO SURVIVE A SHIPWRECK

1. **Scope it out.** Like when you are waiting for an airplane to take off, read the ship's emergency instructions and note the location of the life rafts (and life jackets) before you set sail.

2. **Keep your cool.** If an emergency has happened, and you've made it into a life raft, keep your wits about you. Seeing a wide expanse of water with no land in sight can be scary. If you're with someone else, try to distract one another.

3. **Stay cool.** To prevent heatstroke during the day, keep yourself covered up from the sun as much as possible. If you can, make a tent or shaded area. Keep your clothes on and wet them with seawater to stay cool.

4. **Be a collector.** You may be surrounded by water, but finding drinking water is hard. Your best bet is to collect and drink rainwater. Anything hollow, as well as waterproof fabric shaped into a pouch, can work as a container. Ration your water carefully and drink it in small sips when you need to hydrate.

The SS *American Star* ran aground in the Canary Islands in 1994.

BE AWARE • If you're stranded at sea, here are some signs that land may be nearby: Birds fly back to land at night, so if you see one, follow its lead. Floating driftwood is a good sign land is nearby. So are cumulus clouds. Murky or muddy water means a river mouth could be close. Follow its path, and land could be welcoming you home!

SKYDIVING

It's a special kind of person who takes pleasure in jumping out of a plane and falling to the ground at (literally) breakneck speed. Hopefully, she's also the kind of person who's packing a working parachute. But what do you do if that parachute doesn't open? Stop screaming and read this!

Leisure Activity?

Parachuting didn't become a pastime until after World War II when there were lots of military parachutists and parachutes. The term "skydiver" was coined in the mid-1950s when the first commercial skydiving schools opened for business.

Your First Jump

You have three options when performing your first skydive: The tandem jump is the most popular jump because you are securely harnessed to a professional skydiver—who controls the parachute—for the entire jump. With the Accelerated Freefall (AFF) jump, you have control of your parachute, but there are two skydiving instructors who fly alongside you. During the instructor-assisted deployment (IAD) jump, you perform the jump by yourself, but an instructor opens your parachute for you within a couple of seconds of you jumping out of the plane.

Free Falling

Before a skydiver opens the chute, a free fall happens. A skydiver falling with arms and legs outstretched can reach a speed of about 120 miles (193 km) per hour. That's as fast as going down the big hills on the world's fastest roller coasters. Some skydivers even try to go faster. You can get greater speeds by flattening out your body like you're diving into a pool.

OPPOSITE: Skydivers can jump with each other and build shapes in the air—this is called free falling in formation.

FAST FACT • Although it might look dangerous, skydiving is an extremely safe activity. On average in the past five years, there were only twenty-two fatalities per three million jumps made each year.

HOW TO SURVIVE A PARACHUTE MALFUNCTION

1 **Reserve it.** Now that land is approaching rapidly, you tug on your parachute cord. What if nothing happens? In a sport like skydiving, you need a back-up plan. All skydivers have a reserve chute, so pull that next.

2 **Do the wave.** If the second chute fails, too, wave to a diving companion whose chute has not opened yet.

3 **Link up.** When your companion gets to you, hook arms. Hook your arms into your buddy's chest straps all the way up to your elbows, then grab hold of your own strap.

4 **Hold on!** Now it's time for your buddy to open the chute. So hold on tight.

5 **Exit quickly.** If you land in water, you'll need to get out of your harness quickly. All the unopened parachute fabric in your backpack will start to absorb water and become very heavy.

SNAKES

They slither, hiss, rattle, and bite. They can squeeze you to death and give you a heart attack from fright. With their flexible bodies and unhinging jaws, snakes can inspire fear like few other creatures. Lucky residents of Antarctica, Iceland, Ireland, Newfoundland, and New Zealand don't have to deal with snakes, but everybody else? Look out below!

Fearsome Fangs

Some classic signs that a snake is venomous are a rattle; "catlike," vertical pupils; or a flat, triangular head. Unfortunately, some snakes that look like they are nonvenomous actually are. The most useful advice is to stay away from all snakes! The majority of snakes will not cause you much harm, even if they bite you. However, 10 percent of snakes do deliver poison through their fangs—and some can deliver a deadly dose. Some of the usual suspects include copperheads, cottonmouths, mambas, rattlesnakes, and cobras. Some of these snakes even have a small "pit" between the eye and nostril that senses the heat of their prey, letting the snake know when to strike. If you're unlucky enough to cross paths with a venom dispenser, freeze. Don't throw rocks or poke it with a stick. Back away slowly and keep going.

Hug It Out

Snakes that are constrictors are not venomous, but they can be just as deadly. Some infamous constrictors are boas, pythons, and anacondas. They ambush their prey, hiding and waiting for something delish to go by, then launching a sneak attack. Just as their name suggests, they coil their bodies around their prey and, each time their prey takes a breath, they constrict, or squeeze, their coils just a little tighter. This goes on until the prey can no longer breathe. *Gasp!*

VENOMOUS SNAKES

COBRA

TREE VIPER

RATTLESNAKE

BE AWARE • Although it was once considered a snakebite treatment option, you should not suck the venom from the wound. Not only is doing this ineffective, the venom may enter your bloodstream.

HOW TO TREAT A SNAKEBITE

1 **Get help.** Get medical help immediately. Even bites from non-venomous snakes should be treated.

2 **Clean it out.** Wash the bite with soap and water as soon as you can.

3 **Keep it down low.** Keep the bitten area as still as possible and below the heart. Doing this will help slow the flow of venom in your bloodstream.

4 **Wrap it up.** If you are unable to get medical help within 30 minutes, wrap a bandage 2 to 4 inches (5 to 8 cm) above the bite. Make sure it is not too tight.

5 **Write it down.** If you can, jot down a description of the snake. That will help identify it for proper treatment of the bite.

DON'T RATTLE ME

SPELUNKING

Ever thought about exploring Earth's guts? Spelunkers do it with gusto. Spelunkers are folks who go beneath the Earth's surface on cave explorations to check out mineral formations, closed ecosystems, and paleontological remains. They also frequently encounter bats, gas, and creepy crawlers. So keep in mind: Friends don't let friends spelunk alone.

All Gassed Up

Caves can be poorly ventilated, so it's easy for deadly gasses to collect down there. Cavers call this "bad air." Carbon monoxide (CO) and carbon dioxide (CO_2) are two gasses that threaten spelunkers. Carbon monoxide is particularly dangerous because you can't smell it, taste it, or see it. If you get a headache or start feeling dizzy, these are signs of bad air. That's your cue to cave and head straight for the exit.

Bat-Cave

A colony of bats springing from the depths and flapping their leathery wings can give you quite a fright. They can also give you some nasty diseases if they manage to plant their fangs on you. Bats are known to carry rabies. Fruit bats, found in caves in Africa, can even carry the deadly Ebola virus. If a bat bites you, get it checked out. Even bat breath can be dangerous. It creates carbon dioxide, and enough bats over time can raise the concentration of this gas to toxic levels in caves.

FAST FACT • Spelunkers love exploring ice caves. These crystal palaces are majestic but especially dangerous. During the warmer months, there is a real risk of falling chunks of ice. Always wear a helmet!

Stalagmites are mineral deposits that rise from the floors of limestone caves; stalactites are deposits that hang from these caves' ceilings.

HOW TO SQUEEZE YOUR WAY OUT OF A CAVE

1 **Tighten up.** Caves are filled with narrow passageways, tight crevices, and tough turns called crawls and pinches. Before you try to squeeze through a pinch, make sure all of your clothing is tucked in so that nothing gets snagged. If you are wearing a backpack, take it off, and empty your pockets to make it easier for you to slip by.

EXHALE FULLY.

WIGGLE.

EMPTY POCKETS

2 **Make some wiggle room.** Exhale all of the air from your body to help make you that much smaller to wiggle your way through the passage.

3 **Claw at the walls.** If you do get stuck, don't panic. The walls of a cave are often caked with loose material. Claw and scrape at the wall—you might make a little more room.

4 **Tell your friends.** Let your fellow cavers know if you are stuck. They should be able to help push or pull you through a pinch. Also, be prepared to help others if they get stuck.

SPIDERS

Spiders are predators born with venomous fangs and eight legs (often hairy)—no wonder they are people's number one fear! There are over 50,000 different types of these arachnids, but only twenty-five can actually make humans sick. If you run into one of *those* spiders, you probably shouldn't stay sitting on your tuffet.

Widow Maker

The black widow has the most toxic venom of any spider in North America. She's marked by red dots or hourglass on her swollen black abdomen. This marking makes her easy to spot. She's just a little thing, about ½ inch (13 mm) long, but her venom is fifteen times stronger than the venom of a 5-foot (1.5-m) rattlesnake. Luckily, she doesn't deliver a whole lot of it. Black widow bites are rarely fatal, but they are still very serious.

A female black widow spider spins her sticky web to trap prey.

The Wanderer

Most spiders usually wait for prey to come to them. The Brazilian wandering spider is an exception. This aggressive, fearless spider roams the South American rainforests at night with its 5-inch (15-cm) legs, looking to feast on lizards and mice. During the day, it seeks shade under a log, in a termite mound, or even in a shoe. This spider also hides in banana bunches that sometimes get shipped to other parts of the world. You don't want to find one on your banana. Its venom packs a toxic punch.

FAST FACT • Australian funnel spiders are probably the meanest looking of all arachnids. They have large powerful fangs that can bite right through your shoe or even your toenail. Ouch!

VENOMOUS SPIDERS

Venomous spiders are found around the world.

BLACK WIDOW TARANTULA BRAZILIAN WANDERING SPIDER AUSTRALIAN RED-BACK SPIDER

HOW TO DEAL WITH A TARANTULA

1 **Shake it off.** A tarantula might look like a deadly spider, but its venom isn't much stronger than a bee sting. If one crawls on you, just bounce up and down and shake it off.

2 **Clean and cool.** Tarantulas have large fangs, so their bite can be very painful. If you get bitten, clean the area with soap and water. Then apply an ice cube to the bite to keep the swelling down and help relieve the pain.

3 **Rare reaction.** If you break out in a rash, begin coughing or sneezing, get a headache, or start to feel nauseous, you might be allergic. See a doctor immediately.

4 **Eye the bite.** The biggest threat from a tarantula bite is infection. If the area around the bite becomes red and warm to the touch, or if you see red streaks near the area and yellow fluid oozing from the bite, get it checked out by a doctor.

SURFING

Whether you're a gnarly dude in search of a sick honker or a pale-skinned barney with dings on your twin fin, you know that people have been surfing for over 1,000 years. Though pros make it look easy, one wrong move and you might slurp a **Neptune cocktail** (saltwater) while getting a sand facial. Here's how to hang loose, dude!

Getting Wet

If you want to catch some waves, the first thing you'll need is a surfboard. For beginners, long boards are the way to go. They're more stable and easier to ride than shorter boards. You will also need a leash to keep you from losing your board, and a wetsuit. Apply wax to the face of the surfboard for traction, or you'll just slip right off.

Know the Code

Surfers have a code when it comes to catching waves. In general, the surfer closest to the peak of the wave has the right to ride it. If there is a wave that you can ride in either direction, call out "Left" or "Right" to let other surfers know which direction you intend to take. Trying to ride a wave that someone else is already surfing is called "dropping in." Dropping in is dangerous and not cool! Be patient and wait for a wave to call your own.

Rocky Ending

Surfers call falling off their board a wipeout. The worst wipeouts are ones involving something other than water. Waves often break over sandbars and coral reefs. Always wear a wet suit when you go surfing to minimize the damage. Coral reefs are sharp and can cut you. Know the turf before you surf. Check out the area at low tide and note the locations of potentially dangerous sandbars and reefs.

PROPER STANCE

Push your hips forward, shifting your weight, and the nose of the board will dip. Shift your weight back, and the tail of the board will drop.

Position feet facing across the board, hips forward, arms up, and eyes and head looking forward.

SURF'S UP!

HOW TO HANDLE A WIPEOUT

1 Make some distance. When falling, put some distance between you and your board, so it doesn't injure you.

2 Take a breath. You don't know how long you might be underwater, so try to take a deep breath before you go down.

3 Stay calm. Don't try to resist the power of the wave. Let it spin you around until it releases you.

4 Follow the leash. To find your way back to the surface, follow the leash attached to your surfboard.

The "tube" is what surfers call the hollow part of the wave that they surf through.

TIGERS

A tiger's roar can be heard as far as 2 miles (3.2 km) away—an early warning system that this big cat means business. Bigger than a lion, the tiger is the world's largest kitty. Tigers may be cute, but they can also cover 15 feet (4.5 m) in one leap and have 4-inch (10-cm) teeth!

Two's a Crowd

Tigers are solitary creatures. A mother tiger will hunt with her 2-year-old cubs, but only to teach them the tricks of the trade. Their favorite trick is the sneak attack. Tigers hunt mostly at night, using their stripes for camouflage in tall grass. You might not see a tiger coming, but it will see you. Tigers have night vision that is six times better than yours. Tigers may be lightning quick, but they aren't great distance runners. They only strike when prey is close. But when they do strike, the hunt is over in seconds.

Aqua Kitty

Your pet cat might hate getting wet, but tigers are actually great swimmers. They can swim as far as 18 miles (29 km), and are often found cooling off and relaxing in ponds and rivers. Sometimes they hunt prey in the water and have even been known to attack people on boats.

Rare Breeds

Historically, tigers have killed more people than any other big cat. Attacks are more rare these days, but so are tigers. Of the nine subspecies of modern tigers, three have gone extinct in the last 100 years. In fact, there are fewer than 2,500 tigers left in Asia and the eastern part of Russia.

A Siberian tiger stalks its prey in shallow water.

HOW TO SURVIVE A TIGER ATTACK

1. **Watch your back.** Some tigers actually stalk humans for food. So be alert in tiger territory, like jungles, grasslands, and forests. Don't travel alone, especially at night when tigers are more likely to be on the prowl.

2. **Back it up.** Don't ever run from a tiger. This triggers its predatory instincts. Don't turn your back on a tiger, either. Slowly back away. Tigers like to surprise their prey, so they might abandon a hunt if they lose the element of surprise.

3. **Give it a gag order.** If a tiger takes you down, quickly shove your hand into its mouth and down its throat. Tigers have a strong gag reflex that prevent them from chomping down… at least for a while.

TORNADOS

The sky has turned an eerie greenish-black. And is that a freight train roaring through town? Uh oh! The sky may start raining debris. If you see a rotating funnel cloud, which can be more than 1 mile (1.6 km) wide with winds up to 300 miles (483 km) per hour, grab **Toto** because that's a tornado heading your way!

Twisted Destruction

A tornado twisting through a populated area can tear houses to shreds. Strong tornados can suck cars right off the ground. While getting sucked into the funnel of a tornado is near certain death, most deaths and injuries actually come from the debris.

Mother of All Tornados

When scientists try to predict tornados, they look for "supercells," which are giant thunderstorms with a strong updraft of air. It's this updraft that gives the twister lift. Not all supercells give birth to tornados, but a single supercell can spawn what is called a "tornado family." This is one family you don't want to be a part of.

Professional storm chasers stalk tornados in specially protected vehicles, from which they can take measurements and photos.

HOW TO SURVIVE A TORNADO

1 **Don't get it twisted.** If there is a "Tornado *Watch*" in your area, keep an eye on the sky. If there is a "Tornado *Warning*", that means a tornado has been spotted. Head for shelter and don't look back.

2 **Go low.** In a house, head for the lowest floor, ideally the basement. If you don't have a basement, stay in the middle of the house, away from windows, to protect you from broken glass and flying debris. Put as many walls and barriers between you and the outside as possible. Hide in a closet, beneath a stairwell, or under a sturdy table.

3 **Cover up.** To defend yourself against flying debris, cover up with a blanket or sleeping bag. At the very least, protect your head and neck with your hands.

4 **Move on.** Cars and trucks don't offer much protection. The same goes for mobile homes. Even a modest tornado can cause serious damage to a vehicle. If you are on the road, don't try to outdrive the tornado. Abandon the vehicle and head for shelter.

5 **Ditch it.** If you are caught out in the open, look for a ditch or low-lying area and lie facedown. Cover your head and neck with your arms. Don't seek shelter under a bridge or overpass. The passageway under a bridge can act like a wind tunnel and actually increase the already ferocious wind speeds.

FAST FACT • The small U.S. town of Codell, Kansas, is known for a crazy cyclonic coincidence. Three years in a row, in 1916, 1917, and 1918, this town was hit by a tornado. And all three happened on the same day, May 20!

TSUNAMIS

If you've ever had a monster burp, you probably felt it rumbling deep in your belly before it roared out. A tsunami is Mother Earth's big belch. Starting as an underwater earthquake, a tsunami rapidly produces surging waves that slam shores and destroy everything in their paths. So you better get outta there. Fast.

Why the Waves?

When a tsunami strikes, an earthquake (p. 46) is usually to blame. An underwater landslide or volcanic explosion (p. 130) can also make some mean waves—so can a meteor or asteroid (p. 22). The water captures the frightful energy of the instigator and reaches speeds faster than 500 miles (805 km) per hour at the deepest part of the ocean. That's as fast as a commercial jet.

Wall of Water

Tsunamis have a different appearance in the open water than they do on shore. Some deadly tsunamis are only 1 foot (30 cm) high in deep water. A tsunami can pass under a ship without the people on board noticing. But this modest wave can stretch as long as 1 mile (1.6 km). When it hits the shallows, it slows down and starts to pile up. That's when the killer wave takes shape. The 2004 tsunami is estimated to have soared as high as a seven-story building in some places.

The word "tsunami" comes from the Japanese words *tsu*, meaning "harbor," and *nami*, meaning "wave."

HOW TO SURVIVE A TSUNAMI

1 **Make a run for it.** If the ocean suddenly retreats from the beach, so should you! Frothy water on the horizon and a low rumbling sound are also warning signs.

2 **Head for the hills.** Getting to higher ground is pretty much the only course of action in a tsunami situation. A steel-framed building should be safe—the taller the better. You want to get to the highest floor possible.

3 **Climb a tree.** In a pinch, you can climb a tree. Get as high as you can and wrap your arms and legs around the trunk. Then hold on tight!

4 **Float your boat.** If you are on a boat, you'll have to make a decision. You can go to port and head for higher ground, or you can head for deep water since tsunamis aren't dangerous until they get near shore. Decide quickly, because the tsunami won't wait around while you play "Eeny, Meeny, Miny, Mo!"

FAST FACT · In 2004, Tilly Smith, a ten-year-old British girl, became a hero when she warned beachgoers in Thailand about the approaching tsunami. She had just learned about tsunamis in geography class two weeks earlier and noticed the quickly receding waters. The beach was evacuated safely.

TURBULENCE

You know that stomach-lurching feeling you get on roller coasters? That "goodbye, lunch!" sensation is also what you may feel when experiencing turbulence. This unsettling jostling occurs when two streams of air surrounding a plane flow into each other. Here's how to deal with that little (or big) bump in the sky.

Stress Test

Turbulence can be terrifying. Sometimes it can feel like the plane is falling right out of the sky. Keep in mind that commercial airplanes are built to handle a lot. Even severe turbulence can't damage a plane.

For a smoother ride, try to get a seat over the wing—it may prevent you from having to use that bag.

Wake Up!

The most dangerous turbulence is known as "wake turbulence" and is caused by other airplanes disturbing the air. This type of turbulence often happens during takeoffs and landings. If a plane is high in the sky and takes a little dip, it's no big deal. But if a plane is coming in for a landing and takes an unexpected dip—it's a very big deal. The amount of wake turbulence a plane creates is related to the size of the aircraft. Air traffic controllers try to time the takeoffs and landings to make sure wake turbulence isn't a factor. So the next time you're waiting on a runway annoyed about the delay, remember that waiting around is better than a treacherous takeoff.

Pilots will regularly request permission from air traffic control to go to a higher altitude to avoid turbulence.

HOW TO HANDLE AIRPLANE TURBULENCE

1 **Buckle up.** Even when the seat belt sign is off, it's a good idea to keep your seat belt fastened, in case of surprise turbulence. Unbuckled passengers or those in the bathroom have suffered turbulence-related injuries, ranging from cuts and bruises to concussions and even broken bones. One woman was paralyzed by a broken neck in 2009.

2 **It's all in your head.** Turbulence feels a lot more dangerous than it is. As long as you're buckled up, you should be safe. If you're really rattled, try to distract yourself. Play a video game. Read a book. Watch the in-flight movie. Or strike up a conversation.

3 **Stay focused.** If you can't distract yourself, try staring at a fixed object, like the seat back in front of you. Doing this should help reduce the unsettling sensation.

4 **Bag it.** If you feel sick, use the airsickness bag or, as it's more commonly called, the barf bag. See step 1: You could injure yourself if you try to make it to the bathroom.

When the lurching starts, put your tray table away and hold tight to your stuff.

VOLCANOS

Volcanos not only kill around 850 people a year, but in 2010, the ash from Iceland's easy-to-pronounce volcano, Eyjafjallajökull, was so powerful that it stopped all flights to and from Europe for a week. But Eyjafjallajökull is just one of 1,900 active volcanos worldwide, and any one of them could really mess up your vacation plans (or worse).

The Karymsky is one of many active volcanoes on Russia's Kamchatka Penninsula.

HOW TO SURVIVE A VOLCANIC ERUPTION

1 **Look out above!** If rocks are raining down on you, protect yourself. Roll into a tight ball and cover your head with your hands.

2 **Look out below!** If red-hot lava is headed your way, try to move out of its path as quickly as possible. But don't head for low-lying areas like rivers and valleys. That's where the lava is flowing.

3 **Seek shelter.** Get inside as soon as possible. Close all doors and windows, and move to the highest floor.

4 **Stay standing.** If you're stuck on a lower level, do not sit or lie down on the floor. Volcanic gases are made up of carbon dioxide, a deadly gas. Because it's heavier than air, it accumulates closer to the ground.

Blowing Off Some Steam

When gasses build up beneath the Earth's surface, they eventually have to be released. And when the Earth lets one rip, it's often violent and deadly. Volcanic eruptions can send rocks and debris flying for miles. Volcanos belch giant plumes of poisonous gas and ash into the air. Though the lava might look really dangerous (and it is!), it's actually the toxic gasses and raining ash that cause the most problems for people. The ash might look light and fluffy but it's actually made of rock. Just 1 inch (2.5 cm) of volcanic ash is heavy enough to cause a roof to collapse.

Going Global

The dangers of living near the base of an active volcano are pretty obvious, but major eruptions can actually affect the whole world. The ash and gasses blasted into the sky by a major eruption can block sunlight and lower temperatures across the globe. This is known as "volcanic winter." In 1815, Mount Tambora in Indonesia had the biggest eruption in recorded history. The following year is known as the "Year Without a Summer." Temperatures dropped in Asia, Northern Europe, and North America and caused many crops to fail, leading to food shortages. The year of 1816 is also known as "Eighteen Hundred and Froze to Death."

The molten rock that flows from an erupting volcano can travel many miles before slowing and cooling.

WHITEWATER

If you've ever ridden a log flume at an amusement park and gotten slammed with bubbling whitewater, you have a tiny taste of what it's like to shoot the rapids. Whitewater rapids, usually occurring in rocky, narrow parts of rivers or after a flooding storm, are rough to ride. So whenever you see whitewater, prepare for a wild one.

Head of the Class

Whitewater is ranked on a scale according to how dangerous it is. The scale goes from Class I through Class VI. The lower end is Class I. This means rafters will come across small rough areas. Even rookie rafters can handle it. On the other end, a stretch of Class VI whitewater is *extremely* dangerous. This type of water contains large waves, huge rocks, and horrendous hazards that can rip a raft to shreds. Traveling down Class VI white-water is only for the ultimate experts.

Ready for Rapids

If you are planning to take on the rapids, be prepared. Choose a professional guide. Travel light (there isn't much room on the raft), but know that a helmet, a life jacket, and a first-aid kit are must-haves. Sunscreen, sunglasses, and insect repellent are also important. Even in the summer, bring a warm set of clothes. The water can lower your body temperature during the day, and you will want something warm and dry to wear when the rafting day is done. Be prepared for exercise when you hit the whitewater. You might think the river does all the work, but navigating the rapids takes a lot of tough paddling.

RAFTING GEAR

Be prepared.

HOW TO SURVIVE A TRIP OVER A WATERFALL

1. **Stay upright.** Always go feet first—squeeze your feet together and stay vertical.

2. **Time it.** At the last second, before going over the edge, jump out and away from the waterfall. And take a deep breath.

3. **Cover your head.** You're out there, you're falling, now cover that noggin of yours with your arms.

4. **Swim for it.** Start swimming the second you hit the water, even before you're totally under. Once you're up, swim strongly downstream. You don't want to get trapped behind the waterfall or on the rocks under it.

BE AWARE • If you capsize or get ejected from your watercraft, the safest thing to do is to swim to your friend Eddy. An eddy is a calm spot in the water that is immediately behind a boulder—the current breaks up around the rock. Hang on to the boulder, so you don't get swept downstream.

A raft's low center of gravity makes it a very stable craft.

WOODS

Camping, hiking, picnicking, s'mores—what's not to love about spending time in the woods?! Well, how about unexpected weather (lightning! hail! snow!), injury (sprained ankles! can opener fiascos! stings and bites!), or falling off the beaten path? Fortunately, good prep can prevent the great outdoors from becoming terrifying territory.

Communicate Your Fate

If you are going hiking in the woods, especially alone, tell at least three people about your plans. Let them know that if they do not hear from you by a certain time, they should put an emergency plan into action to find you.

The Whole Kit and Caboodle

Even if you're going on a short hike, bring a survival kit with you. Include a map detailing the hiking trails. Bring extra layers of clothing, including a waterproof layer. A garbage bag is light, compact, and can serve multiple purposes, including waterproofing. Food and water are essential. Bring a small pot for collecting and boiling water. A whistle, sunscreen, insect repellent, waterproof matches, a smart phone with GPS, an all-purpose knife, and a rope should also go in the kit, along with first-aid supplies. This may seem like a lot, but if you get into trouble, you'll be glad you have it.

Hot Stuff

Spending an unexpected night in the woods can be a chilling experience. If you are unprepared, you can improvise a warmer outfit by stuffing dry leaves under your clothes. Alternatively, if you brought a garbage bag along with you, you can stuff this with dry leaves and then crawl inside like it's a sleeping bag.

FIELD GUIDE

For a sprained ankle, tear a T-shirt into strips that are 4 inches (10 cm) wide. Wrap the ankle like a figure eight, up over the ankle and back around the foot. If a cold creek is nearby, soak your ankle before wrapping to keep the swelling down. Use a strong piece of wood as a walking stick.

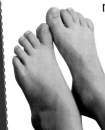

HOW TO SURVIVE GETTING LOST IN THE WOODS

1 **Backtrack.** As soon as you realize you are lost, stop right where you are. Time to backtrack and retrace your steps as closely as possible. If you find a marked trail along the way, follow it, even if it's not the one you started on.

2 **Blaze your way.** While you're backtracking, blaze your own trail by breaking small branches and turning over rocks. This will help others find you if you become hopelessly lost. It will also let you know if you are walking in circles.

3 **Holler back.** Shout, "HELP!" along the way and listen for a response. If you have a whistle, give it three long toots frequently.

4 **Stay put.** Don't backtrack too long. If you haven't found the trail you started on after a certain amount of time, chances are you're walking in the wrong direction. Find a good spot, such as under a sturdy tree or near a water source, and stop moving altogether.

INDEX

Illustrations are in *italics*.

PHOTO CREDITS

ABOUT THE EXPERTS

Charlie Maciejewski is the head of the Social Studies Department at the Kurt Hahn Expeditionary Learning School in New York City. He encourages students to question what they thought was possible by engaging them in learning adventures, including doing tai chi in Chinatown, walking blindfolded over the Brooklyn Bridge, rappelling down steep walls, and working at urban farms. In his spare time, Charlie loves to hang with his two Siamese cats, ride his bike, snowboard, and take deep breaths. On one of his adventures, Charlie encountered a bear: keeping his cool, he slowly backed away and survived to review this book and go on more adventures!

Carmelo Piazza, AKA "Carmelo the Science Fellow," is known throughout Brooklyn, New York, for his popular after-school science classes and science birthday parties, held at The Cosmic Cove. Carmelo has a Bachelor's degree in elementary education and a Master's degree in environmental science. He has been teaching science to elementary schoolkids at PS 261 for twelve years, and at The Cosmic Cove since 2005. His students like to say, "His favorite color is yellow, he likes to eat cherry Jell-o, and he looks like a big marshmallow."

Lisa Polak is a scientist with degrees in animal biology and molecular genetics who has worked as an animal researcher and handler for more than fifteen years. She currently works in research at The Rockefeller University in New York City, and is a volunteer and animal handler at the Prospect Park Zoo in Brooklyn, NY. Lisa's most extreme animal encounter was when she accidentally disturbed a wasp nest in the jungle in Costa Rica and received three stings between the eyes. Ouch!

ABOUT THE AUTHORS & ILLUSTRATOR

David Borgenicht is a the creator and co-author of all the books in the WCSSH series. His has encountered snakes, mountain lions, and bulls in his life—but not komodo dragons! There is still time, however. He lives in Philadelphia with his wife and two children, who are his greatest adventures.

Molly Smith is a writer and editor who has survived many worst-case scenarios, including being trapped on a balcony with a swarm of bees, a standoff with two wild turkeys, and being mobbed everywhere she goes by her adoring readers. Most impressive, however, is how she survived growing up with her not-so-little brother Brendan Walsh. Molly lives in Connecticut.

Brendan Walsh is a freelance writer from the Boston area whose run-ins with the worst case include a surprise skunk attack, a brush with a mean riptide, and a bite from a venomous (though unidentified) spider that made his arm swell up like a balloon.

Robin Epstein vividly recalls getting squirted in the eye with *extremely* hot jalapeno pepper juice in middle school. When her vision finally returned, she was never so happy to see a cafeteria lunch lady.

Chuck Gonzales is a New York City–based illustrator who was raised in South Dakota. He's no stranger to worst cases, having illustrated *The Worst-Case Scenario Survival Handbook: Junior Edition*. Growing up in the Dakotas, he is very familiar with surviving on the tundra.